GOD's Hand In My Life

Carlton Carney

Printed in the United States of America.

Library of Congress Control Number: 2019932775

ISBN	Paperback	978-1-64361-219-5
	Hardback	978-1-64361-375-8
	eBook	978-1-64361-220-1

Westwood Books Publishing LLC
10389 Almayo Ave, Suite 103
Los Angeles, CA 90064

www.westwoodbookspublishing.com

Contents

Preface v

Foreword vii

Early Years (1935-1941) 1
- My Birth 1
- My Mother 1
- My Bowed Legs 3
- My Father 3
- The Ashland Home 8

Growing Up (1941-1953) 20
- Mars Hill 20
  - First Home 21
  - Second Home 25
- After Graduation 44

Military (1954-1959) 48
- Basic Training 48
- Military Training 50

Martin-Marietta (1959-1962) 59
- Titan Missile Training Development 59
- Wichita Falls 65
- Site Technical Representative 67

Radio And Tv Repair (1961-1963) 69

Philco Technical Representative (1963) 72
- Pamela 73

Move To Minnesota (1963) 77

Control Data (1963- 1987) 79
First House 80
Large Programs Management 93
Small Farmer Program 100
Second House 101
Multi-Media Products 104
1987 105
Carney Associates (1987- 2000) 109
Honeywell (1988-1989) 112
Selling House (1993-1994) 114
Rush City Home (1994) 116
Grand Casino Project (1996-1997) 118
Teaching At Local Colleges (1997-2000) 119
Retirement (2000-2017) 121
Medical Problems (2002) 121
Shepherds Chapel (2004) 123
Pam's Death (2014) 124
Restoration Church (2014) 127
Chisago City (2015) 131
Music Trivia (2015) 133
Forest Lake (2016-2017) 134
Summary 137
Endnotes 141

Preface

I want to begin by removing any misconceptions. I do not believe I am special in any way, far from it. This story is presented out of great humility. Why the Lord, God, has been a friend throughout my life shows his great love and grace. A human friend would have abandoned me long ago.

Originally, I began writing about my childhood experiences with the intention of providing my children a description of life back then. Over a period of a couple years I would add a bit, and then leave it for a while. When I had the document through high school, I stopped writing and forgot about it for about 20 years. It was called: "A Story About Carlton" at that time. It had accomplished my original intentions so I was content to leave it as it was.

Over a year ago, I discovered the document and felt a drive to expand the "story" and to focus it on God's involvement; which, as I looked back, seemed to be throughout my life. It was no longer a story about me, so the title had to change. I mentioned to my daughter, Sally, one day about the book and that I was wrestling with a title when she said, "How about: God's Hand In My Life?" That captured my intent very well. The story had become a book.

My purpose in writing this book is first and foremost as a testimonial to the great love and compassion the Lord has shown me over and over. It is with hope that what I say in this book brings comfort and strength to the reader. The second reason for this book is to provide a glimpse of what life was like in my childhood, which was so much different from today's world. The third reason is to capture, as best I can, the transitions that occurred during my life, thereby showing the Lord's leading, even though I was unaware most of the time.

I must admit that there has been the temptation, throughout this writing, to emphasize my accomplishments. I will be the first to admit that I have been fortunate to have had a wonderful and interesting work experience. If I were to admit otherwise, I would not be truthful. At the same time, being equally truthful, I would have to admit that the Lord was behind that experience; and so He deserves the credit.

I want to be sure that I do not leave any wrong impressions concerning Christian denominations. I began as a Catholic and though I changed to eventually becoming nondenominational, I feel that was appropriate for me. This fact, however, should not cause the reader to think that I believe that specific Christian denominations are in some ways inferior. My parents, my sister, and my older brothers were Catholics throughout their lives. When looking for churches to go to during my life, I went to several denominational churches. In the BSF groups I lead were people from many denominations. I believe that your choice of a church is very personal and must satisfy your spiritual needs.

When mentioning specific individuals in my life; except for family and some friends, I have avoided or changed names to prevent any possible embarrassments or repercussions.

Foreword

You never know what might happen at a Saturday evening church service in a small rural town at a church unassociated with any specific denomination. People walk in off the street, sometimes on the way to a night out at a local bar (or maybe on the way home from that same bar). They might come in after having been at work all day or after an argument with a spouse or child. Sometimes they only come on a Saturday night because they don't want to get up at the crack of dawn to get to "regular" church the next morning. The reasons people come to a Saturday evening church service are as varied as the people themselves.

One night an older, rather distinguished gentleman walked in just as the service was starting. He didn't sit in the back of the church as so many will do. He walked right up, close to the front—but not too close—and sat down. I could see him listening intently. It was obvious by the way he responded to the order of service that this wasn't a new experience. When it came time for our regular open prayer, I, as the pastor, would ask if anyone had anything they would like to add to our prayer list. Carlton Carney spoke up right away. He knew who it was who could help him and hear his prayer request. I believe that he felt comfortable enough, even as a first time visitor, to seek prayer to Jesus Christ through a group of total strangers, connected only by a common faith in the One who sees all and knows all and answers all prayer

That night, through tears, he spoke of having just recently suffered a devastating loss. We prayed for him; that God would take away the hurt and restore the joy that I have come to know is borne deep within this man. I have come to know Carlton as a trusted and devoted friend. I was privileged to be given a very early copy of this book and insight into a most remarkable life. As I read it I was amazed at the life this man has led. His memory of events of nearly 80 years ago is astounding. He has been a part of events that were world changing. But most remarkable, never does Carlton seek his own praise or his own glory or his own notoriety. He will always point to the Lord Jesus Christ as the giver and sustainer of all good things, even many great things.

I believe that after reading this book I have not only been given a glimpse into a life well lived, but an encouragement to remember my own story and to look for God's Hand in *My* Life.

Cary Johnson
Pastor, Restoration Church
SDG

Early Years (1935–1941)

MY BIRTH

I was told it was a blustery day when I came into this world on April 30, 1935. I was not born in a hospital or medical clinic, like is so common today, but rather in a bedroom of our rural home in Ashland, Maine. I had already been preceded by my brother Richard (Dick), by brother John Junior (who died from pneumonia two years after birth), sister Elizabeth (Liz) and brother Warren (Buck). And I would be followed by brothers Dennis and Vincent (Vin).

I don't recall the house I was born in because we moved to another rural house a year or two after I was born. It was this second house that I recall from my early youth.

MY MOTHER

My mother was Lena Helena Bastarache, of French-Canadian decent. She had come to the U. S. from Canada when she was 16. She was short, at only four feet eleven inches tall, a heavy woman and very strong. It was her task to take care of the household and to discipline us kids whenever that was necessary.

She was a hard worker who, like many of the rural women of this time, had a multitude of talents and seldom complained. In addition to cooking, cleaning the house and washing clothes, she canned food, made preserves, crocheted, knitted and even made rugs. She could take raw wool, card it, spin it, dye it and convert it into a variety of clothes from stockings and mittens to sweaters, scarves and hats. She was also creative, making quilts and hook rugs.

I remember her making a hook rug from scraps of material she had prepared for the task. The rug was oval shaped, about three feet wide by six or seven feet long. She said she was going to have a dog in the middle of the rug. She showed me a picture of the dog from a magazine. When the rug was finished, she had the dog centered and it looked like the picture.

Just in the task of washing clothes, it meant filling a tub with hot, soapy water, rubbing the clothes on a washboard that laid against the tub side and descended into the water, refilling the tub with fresh water, rinsing the clothes, squeezing the water out of the clothes by placing them between two rubber rollers which were turned with a handle and then carried out to a clothes line and hung out to dry.

Very little went to waste back then. Whenever Mom and Dad would butcher a hog, they would use just about every part of the hog for something. Besides bacon, ham and various pork cuts, there was pickled pigs feet, head cheese and blood sausages. Some of these I liked and some I didn't

All of our pastries and desserts were made from scratch. Mom made bread in the form of loaves, rolls and biscuits; she also made cupcakes, cookies, pies and cakes. One of my favorite was an apple-filled cookie. Her cakes had thick, hard frosting. I would remove the frosting from the cake, eat the cake and then slowly eat the frosting, savoring every nibble. It was like having a candy treat after eating the delicious cake.

She made a candy in the winter that she called "snow candy." She would cook some kind of a sweet glazed liquid which she would spread on new-fallen snow. It hardened into a shiny, sweet candy that resembled peanut brittle without the peanuts. It had sharp edges and could cut your mouth, if you were not careful eating it. You were supposed to let the piece melt in your mouth but, eager to consume the candy more quickly, I usually carefully chewed it, once in a while cutting my mouth.

One time when we had a group of relatives over for a Sunday dinner, she made strawberry ice cream. I had never had ice cream before (except the last day of school in Ashland when I had ice cream bars on a stick). It was the most delicious thing I had ever eaten.

MY BOWED LEGS

My mother said I was born with very bowed legs. By the time I was eighteen months old, the legs gave me considerable pain at night, especially if I was on my feet during the day. Mother said that she tried to keep me down during the day but whenever I saw the other kids playing; I just had to run out and participate. She would drag me back, but a few minutes later I was at it again.

Mom said that the outlook concerning my legs was bleak because the bones were so badly bent. At my bedtime, my legs would ache from the day's activities, and I would cry until I fell asleep. My mother said she prayed and rocked and prayed and rocked some more until I fell asleep. She said she was told that if my legs didn't straighten out by the time I was two years old, they would be put into metal braces which I would wear the rest of my life. A week before the braces were to be put on, her prayers were answered. Almost overnight my legs straightened, with only a slight bow in them, and the pain had disappeared. *God's hand in my life.*

MY FATHER

My father, John Felix Carney, was born in Ashland, Maine. He was the second-oldest in a family of sixteen (many of whom died at birth.) He had an older sister, Elizabeth, and younger sisters Celina, Delphine, Mary and Pauline, with a brother Peter, born between Delphine and Mary. Dad's parents were Peter Carney and Delina Adelaide Beaulieu, both of French-Canadian decent. We called them Grampy and Grammy.

Figure 1. Grampy, Edgar Hughes and Grammy

Figure 2. Vincent, Mom, Dad and Grammy (1955)

My Dad said that Grampy had been a woodsman who would go out with a crew of lumberjacks for six months at a time, living in a log building consisting of a large room with a wood-stove kitchen, large dining table and bunkbeds lining the walls. As his family grew, Grampy needed help in providing the necessary income to support his family. Dad was the oldest boy and had gone to school for a couple of years; when, at nine years old, he had to join Grampy in the woods.

Dad's first job at the camp was what was called a "Cookee". He helped the chef prepare meals, and would do various chores around the camp, such as bringing in wood for the stove, washing dishes and cleaning. He was taught how to cook the various meals and desserts. As time went on he expanded his learning to sharpening saws, splitting wood and, later, became a lumberjack himself. Dad was unusually strong and was able to do the work of much older men. He was also very competitive and would force himself to keep up with the other men.

At around eighteen, Dad was offered the job of cook at a hotel in Bangor that his brother-in-law, Walter Brooks (his sister Elizabeth's husband), had purchased. The story was that Walter had made considerable money during the prohibition of liquor by selling bootlegged booze which he had smuggled in from Canada. By the time the prohibition ended, Walter was a rich man and invested his money in the purchase of a large hotel in Bangor. Mom was staying with two aunts who lived near the Bangor area. They heard that Walter was looking for someone to clean the hotel rooms, so she ended up at the hotel working for Walter. This is where Mom and Dad met and eventually got married.

As his family began to grow, Dad decided to become a farm hand. Times were getting hard and he reasoned that, working for a farmer provided some income as well as free food. He moved back to Ashland where the farms in that area grew primarily potatoes. He would work the fields from spring planting to late summer. In the fall he opted to pick potatoes rather than dig them, because he could earn a lot more money. In the winter he worked in a potato house sorting and packaging potatoes to fill orders.

Picking potatoes back then was a tough job. In northern Maine, potatoes are grown in rows. A tractor would pull a two-row digger (some farmers had one-row diggers often pulled by a horse) that cut deep into the bottom of the rows, lifting potatoes, tops, rocks and whatever else might be there, onto a rotating bed of metal rods that would literally shake the dirt loose. Dirt and smaller objects would fall between the rods back to the ground while larger objects, like potatoes and larger rocks, would ride the rods and be deposited on top of the fallen dirt.

A field would be marked off into sections, with each picker remaining within his or her section. Fast pickers would have longer sections than slow pickers. The idea was to provide enough space for all pickers to remain busy all day and complete the day's work at about the same time.

Potatoes were picked into wooden baskets that varied in size from a peck (ten to twelve pounds) to a bushel (30 to 40 pounds). You selected the basket size to suit your strength. When a basket was full of potatoes, it was hand-carried and dumped into a wooden barrel. Pickers were paid by the full barrel. Pickers had unique identification stiff-paper tags that they would put onto the tops of their full barrel to identify the barrel as theirs. Fast pickers could pick over 100 barrels a day, but the average was more like 60 to 80 a day for an adult picker.

Barrels were loaded onto a truck using a winch and grappling hook that would lift them onto the truck bed. The tags were collected from each barrel at this time. Once the truck was loaded, the driver would deliver the barrels to a potato house. These were long buildings having huge below-ground storage bins to hold the potatoes for later packaging and marketing. The bins provided a dark, cool environment to keep the potatoes fresh and sprout-free for months at a time. At the end of the week, potato pickers were paid twenty-five cents for each tag collected.

Picking potatoes meant either standing and bending, or kneeling. I preferred standing; others preferred kneeling. My Dad would do both; standing part of the time and kneeling at other times, to give his back a rest. Even though my mother sewed pads onto the knees of my workpants, I still didn't like kneeling because the rocks bruised my knees. I guess I preferred bruised knuckles to bruised knees.

I remember we would go out to the potato fields each day before sunrise, remaining there until sunset. This would continue until all of the farmer's potatoes were picked, usually a two to three week period. There would be a one-hour break for lunch at about noon each workday. Equipment breakdown, which was frequent, and rain, would stop all harvesting. When Dennis and I were young, the noon break and quitting times were our favorite times of the day. Our favorite song while we were picking was: "Let It Rain and Let It Snow." A favorite rhyme was: "Let It Rain, Let It Pour, Let the Old Man Snore." Whenever Dennis and I saw a single cloud in the sky, we would start singing the song or say the rhyme. We had little motivation to pick potatoes at that time. That changed, though, when we were older and realized how much money we could make during this brief, but strenuous period.

Our purpose in being in the fields when we were young was not to earn money so much as to enable our parents to earn money; if we picked potatoes, so much the better. The main task was to stay out of trouble, which we usually did, but not always.

Dad was unusually strong. Although he was six feet, one inch tall and weighed about 190 pounds, he was much stronger than he looked. He was also very competitive. In 1936 there was a world's champion potato picking and barrel rolling contest in Springfield, Massachusetts. He won both contests. When it came to competing, he was aggressive.

Dad didn't like chain saws when they first came out. He thought they were loud, smoky and not as good at cutting wood as a skilled person with a saw. One time he competed against the chain saw with a buck saw on television in Bangor. His competitor was having trouble getting his saw going and Dad would crack a joke, making fun of the saw. They were to make two cuts through a six-inch log. When they finally got competing, Dad was through both logs when his competitor was just beginning his second cut.

Dad was a story teller and everyone he knew enjoyed his stories. Most of the stories were made up about someone. He had stories about his favorite uncle, Nun, one of his Dad's brothers. Apparently, he must have gotten negative feedback at some point in time because from then on all of his stories were about Felix. He told me one time that he chose Felix because it was his middle name and if anyone complained, he could say that the story was about himself.

Later he would work for Simonds Saw and Steel Company as a representative. He traveled all over New England visiting saw mills, doing troubleshooting and sales. He worked out of his home but once in a while he would go into the company. Whenever he was there, company executives would invite him into their meeting so he could tell them one of his stories.

One of his Felix jokes was when Felix was working as a lumberjack at a camp in the woods. There would be a crew of a dozen or more men living there for months at a time cutting pulpwood. This time there was a professional wrestler who joined the crew to stay in shape during the wrestling off season. One day they had completed their quota early and everyone was standing around the yard talking. The wrestler challenged Felix to a wrestling match. Felix was husky and strong, but had never wrestled before. The boss of the camp was going to be the referee and told the two not to do any dirty holds. He said that if anyone wanted to give up, all they had to say was the word, "Sufficient."

They began wrestling and poor Felix was being pummeled and put into various holds, but didn't say a word. The wrestler got Felix in a hammerlock. Felix's face turned red, but not a word came out of his mouth. Finally, the wrestler slipped and Felix got a leg hold around the wrestler's waist. His powerful legs made it impossible for the wrestler to breath. Gasping for air, the wrestler yelled, "Sufficient!"

Felix released his hold, looked at the boss and said, "There's that damn word I've been trying to think of!"

Dad was bilingual, having grown up in a French-speaking family, but also learning to speak English very well from his brief schooling. As part of his touring of New England as a Simons representative, he would take in lumberjack contests of various kinds. This one Saturday Dad took me with him to Vermont where they were having a lumberjack contest. We stepped out of the car to hear a French-Canadian trying to explain a problem he was having with his saw. His English was atrocious. Dad walked up to him and started speaking French. The man did a double-take and with a fascinating look asked Dad, "How you could told I been French? You make a good detekative." Dad smiled and said in French, "It was just a lucky guess."

THE ASHLAND HOME

The house we lived in from the time I was three until six years old was a farm house about three miles north of Ashland on the Frenchville Road. The house was basically a frame with a kitchen, living room and two bedrooms, no electricity, no central heating and no plumbing. The house was owned by Edgar Hughes for whom Dad worked. In addition to farming, Edgar was a close family friend. The house was provided free of rent as long as Dad worked for Edgar. There was a well with a hand pump about 100 feet toward the front of the house, near the gravel road. The outhouse was located in a side-extension of a newly-built garage, about 50 feet toward the rear of the house. Heat for the house came from a large white-pearl and cast iron wood cook stove in the kitchen. Mom and Dad stayed in one bedroom, Dick, Liz and Buck in the second bedroom, while Dennis and I would sleep in the unfinished attic.

Dad had put down some boards on the rafters in the attic, and then Mom had placed a blanket on the boards and a very heavy hand-made thick quilt on top. When Dennis and I went to bed, we would struggle to get under the heavy quilt, but it was so good at keeping us warm.

The house had no insulation. In the summer it was too hot and, in the winter, it became very cold when the cook stove burned its last bit of fuel for the day. It was not uncommon for Dennis and I to see frost on the nails poking through the attic walls and roof when Mom came to get us in the morning.

My Dad was always the first one up. He would get the cook stove going. Once we felt the heat coming up into the attic, Mom would soon get us down to the warm kitchen. My first chore each morning was to go and get two pails of water from the hand pump. I was very strong and had no problem fetching the water. After breakfast I would get two more pails of water unless it was Monday, when I would continue bringing water until the double copper boiler on the stove had the water needed. The extra water was heated for doing the clothes wash and other domestic chores.

When I was five I went to the Ashland public school. There was no kindergarten at this time, so I started in the first grade. The road that passed our house, going toward Ashland from Frenchville, sloped gradually down, crossed a bridge over a small brook, and then went up a long, steep grade. At the top of the steep grade was a house where Buck and I would walk to and await the school bus. The old couple who lived there was very hospitable and didn't mind us waiting inside. On bitter cold mornings, it was great having a warm place to wait for the bus. This was the last stop for the bus coming from town. By having us walk to the top of the steep hill, the bus driver didn't take the risk of getting stuck in winter.

Back then, the road would become snow-packed and slippery after a snow storm. This was not a heavily-traveled road so it didn't get the attention of other roads. It was not unusual for the hill to be covered with ice most of the winter. This was not all bad. For us kids, it was an ideal place to slide. One of the fun things was when my brother, Dick, and sister, Liz, along with some friends would drag a large bobsled to the top of the hill, pile on six or more kids and let go. Most of the kids would fall off as the sled went down the hill. It was cold, but we had lots of fun.

I had a sled with metal runners that would pick up a lot of speed down that hill. Buck got a double runner the last winter there. That would hold two people and go even faster than my sled. The way the road went, if we had the right conditions, we could go from the top of the steep hill, past the small grade by our house, then down a long, long hill; a total of about 3 miles or so all the way to Frenchville without stopping. The problem, of course, was the very long walk back.

Buck was the daredevil in the family. He would find a large truck tire and had Dennis and I hold the tire upright while he inserted himself inside the tire. He would have us roll the tire with him inside. If we didn't roll fast enough, the tire would fall, but he would not get hurt. Usually the tire would roll some distance before falling. Buck enjoyed the rides. One time, after several unsuccessful attempts, Buck had me roll the tire to the top of the hill on the gravel road overlooking the bridge and stream below. He insisted on riding the tire down the hill. We got the tire in the center of the road. Buck got into the tire and we began rolling it down the hill. After we took a few steps, the increased momentum took the tire out of our hands and Buck was on his way going toward the bridge. The tire picked up a lot of speed, and remained upright. As it headed toward the bridge, a rock in the road made the tire turn a bit to the left. From our perspective, it looked like he was going to go off the bridge into the water. If he ended up in a deep spot in the water, he could drown. Anticipating the worse, Dennis and I began running down the hill after Buck and the tire. As luck would have it, the tire went off the far end of the bridge and landed on shore. Buck was a little bruised but thought it was the greatest ride he had ever had. He wanted to do it again, but, with no interest in tempting Fate, I would not agree. He was disappointed, but not angry. He talked about the "ride" all the way home.

We raised our own chickens and always had a couple roosters as well. One rooster, a big white one, was really mean and would always take after Dennis. Dennis complained to Mom and Dad, but nothing was done until one day the foolish rooster attacked Dad. We had rooster for Sunday dinner that week.

Dad was a good provider. During the Depression there were times when he worked for fifty cents a day, just to put food on the table. No job was below his dignity. He would clear land for farmers. I asked him one time what was the heaviest thing he ever lifted. He said he had been clearing a field of tree stumps and had removed them all but one. It was a huge stump he had been working on over a month. Whenever he had spare time, he would go and hack away at the stump roots with an axe. He finally got the stump loose, but it was getting late so he decided to come back another day to remove it.

The day he got to the stump to remove it, there had been a shower early that morning. When he got to the stump, the loose ground around the stump was soggy. He backed the pickup to the stump and began wrestling the stump onto the bed of the pickup. He said it was much harder because of the mud. He eventually got the stump onto the pickup and drove to the potato house where he also worked. He and some other men put the stump onto the scale. He said it weighed 735 pound! He said it may not have been the heaviest thing he ever lifted, but because of the mud, it was the hardest thing.

Dad said he was working in the potato house during the winter filling orders for potatoes. Orders would come in for various sizes. The largest containers they filled were 100-pound burlap bags. When they got the bag full, they would tie off the top to seal it, forming what they called "ears" where the burlap extended beyond each end of the bag. One day they had completed their orders early when his fellow workers challenged Dad to show them how much he could lift. He was reluctant at first, but they kept egging him on. He told them if they each put twenty dollars into a pot, he would carry 700 pound of potatoes. Eager to see this, each of the five men put twenty dollars into the pot (some in the form of I.O.U.s). Dad told them to take two one-hundred-pound bags of potatoes and sew the "ears" of the bags together to make a handle so that with one hand he could lift 200 pounds of potatoes. He had them do that again, so there were two sets of bags tied together.

There was a 12-inch wide plank across the potato bin that was used to cross over from one side to the other, rather than walk around the perimeter. He was to walk across the plank to earn his money. He had the men put a one-hundred-pound bag of potatoes on each of his shoulders and another across the top of his head to keep the bags on his shoulders from moving. He then picked up each two hundred pounds of potatoes, making a total of seven hundred pounds, and started across the plank. He said he got about a quarter of the way across and the plank broke from all the weight. He never said if he collected the money, but he was proud to have carried all that weight.

The farm house originally had a barn that had given way to the years. The barn had been torn down and a new, smaller barn had been built in its place. The new barn was about 50 feet diagonally back from the house. There was an extension to the side of the barn toward the house. This extension was closed in and had a 2-seat outhouse, making it a long, cold walk on a winter's night.

The summer before we moved, Dennis and I were playing out behind the barn. There were leftover boards, hay and paper scattered in the area from the recent construction. Dad was working a potato field nearby. He had a tractor and a 500 gallon sprayer which was used to spray potato plants with fertilizer or DDT, depending upon the need. I got the brilliant idea of starting a bonfire. Dennis said not to do it and reminded me that we were not to play with matches, but I would have none of that. I took a match from the kitchen and went behind the barn and pulled together some straw and paper into a small pile, totally ignoring all the surrounding straw, paper and wood.

I lit the fire and before I knew it, it had gone beyond my little pile and was quickly spreading. We both tried stomping it out, but a light breeze kept spreading the flames. Dennis ran to get Mom, while I kept trying to put it out. Dad saw the fire and came with the tractor. He simply drove over the fire with the sprayer on and put the fire out in a hurry. Mom also showed up with a couple pails of water. I figured this was a good time to make my exit. I went to the kid's bedroom where Mom had been cleaning. She had the large cotton-filled mattress that Dick, Liz and Buck slept on, rolled up in the corner of the room. I crawled into the center of the rolled-up mattress and told Dennis to get out of the room and not to tell where I was. Five minutes later

Mom and Dad pulled me out of the mattress and Mom gave me a good spanking. Needless to say, I never played with matches again.

The fire did serve a good purpose. Dad had been meaning to clean up the mess behind the barn and that weekend, he pulled all the debris a good distance away from the barn and burned it. There's something that fascinates me about a fire and watching that big one was a real treat. I had to watch it standing up since my bottom was still sore from the spanking a few days earlier.

Dennis is a year and a half younger than I and, being close in age, we played together a lot. During the summer we went everywhere outside barefooted. There was competition almost all the time, like seeing who could run faster or beat the other at some activity. I remember that attached to the house was a tar-paper shed where firewood was stored. Some of the tar paper was torn, exposing the bare boards underneath. Dennis and I would often climb the wall of the shed by putting our toes and fingers in the cracks between the boards. It was probably 8 or 10 feet to the roof.

Since we had no toilet in the house, we had a wooden bucket that was used by family members who didn't want to venture to the outhouse at night. First thing every morning, Mom would bring the bucket out behind the shed and set it there until she made the trek to the barn to feed the animals, at which time she would then take the bucket and dump it in the outhouse.

This one morning, Dennis and I were playing outside and eventually got around to the shed wall. I started climbing the wall and Dennis was climbing too, trying to beat me. In his haste he fell off about half way up and landed butt first directly in the bucket of sewage. He wasn't hurt but was crying from the humiliation. I thought it was one of the funniest things I had ever seen. Dennis had an unscheduled bath that day.

A moment of reflection here as I think about my mother. An incident like this one with Dennis, and there were many more involving all of us at one time or other, had to have added greatly to her daily tasks, yet I never heard her complain about her chores or her life. She would be understandably upset, but would modify her schedule to accommodate these unexpected events. She had a kind and compassionate heart. None of us kids was a favorite, for she loved and treated all of us equally. She also had a great sense of humor; able to laugh at herself when something happened to her that seemed funny. I remember one time when I was about twelve years old. I was helping her cut some green beans for dinner. She had gotten a cup of tea, which she sipped on while we cut the beans. At one point, when she took a sip of tea, something happened that caused the tea to gush out of her nose. She looked at me and started to laugh, which caused me to laugh. Hers was no ordinary laugh, but a deep and continuous one, raising her hand and slapping her leg. These laughs happened on different occasions. Perhaps they were psychological releases for her laborious lifestyle.

One summer morning Dennis and I were in the barn when this large thing we had never seen before flew out and went down under the bridge over the brook. It was dark in color and flew like a big butterfly. We followed our "butterfly" and found it attached to a beam under the bridge. We got fairly close to it before it flew away. It certainly didn't look like any butterfly we had ever seen. That evening at dinner we mentioned it and were told that our butterfly was a bat.

One of our favorite places to play was by the brook. We often fished or just walked along the bank to see what we could see. Quite often we would see frogs and garter snakes as well as fish. The brook was not very deep, maybe a foot or so in places and three feet or so in others. We had never gone up or down stream more than a few hundred feet until one day when Buck was with us. We decided to go up stream to see where the water came from. About a mile along the brook we came to another bridge.

Off this bridge, the water was deep, maybe six feet or more. When we got to the top of the bridge, we found green and white chemical spills. This is where farmers would fill their sprayers with water and add in fertilizers or DDT. Near the edge of the bridge we found a white thing that looked like a donut, but all donuts we had ever seen were brown. Buck was always good at making up stories to get one of us to do something first. This time he said that what we found was a special donut that was covered with candy. He goaded me to go ahead and take a bite, which I did. As soon as my face lit up, the two of them grabbed the donut and finished it. What we had found was a powdered sugar donut. Unbeknownst to us, it could have been covered with lime or some other white chemical.

A short time after finding the powdered sugar donut, Dennis and I were at the brook and we noticed some dead fish float by. We thought that this was easy fishing so I sent him home to get some empty jars that Mom used for preserves. He brought back a bunch of jars in a little wagon. We picked up the dead fish as they came by and put them in the jars. When we finally got tired of this we had filled eleven quart-size jars with dead brook trout. We proudly brought them all home in the little wagon and presented them to Mom and Dad, thinking we'd have plenty of fish to eat for a long time to come.

Dad got concerned and went to the brook to see for himself. He then went to all the farmers in the area and told them that they were being careless with their fertilizers and killing the fish in the brook. They all became more careful and dead fish were no longer a problem. Mom took the dead fish and buried them in the garden. She said they would make good fertilizer.

Although most of the fish in the brook were six inches or less, once in a while we would see larger ones. One day when Buck, Dennis and I were at the bridge, we noticed a big fish (probably 12 inches or so) that was in a small, deep pool off the bridge. It had somehow gotten there and wasn't able to get out except through shallow water. All three of us were desperate to get the fish so we started getting rocks from a pile on the opposite bank. We would run across the road to the rock pile, pick up a rock, run back across the road and throw the rock at the fish, hoping to kill it that way.

Although Buck was three years older than I, I was stronger. Being really motivated, I was seeking out larger rocks to throw. This one time I found a very large, flat rock. Buck had just thrown a rock and had turned around to get another. I couldn't wait to get to the edge of the road, so I let fly with the big rock when I was half-way across the road. The rock hit Buck in the nose and knocked him out cold. Dennis got Mom who revived Buck with cold water from the brook. There was blood all over. We explained what had happen. I was given a stern talking to about being more careful. Buck had a broken nose but was otherwise fine. When we finally thought to check on the fish, we found it gone. It probably figured that crossing the shallows to a deeper place downstream was better than getting clobbered by our rocks.

That summer before we moved (I was five) Dennis and I started rolling car tires as a toy. I had an old tire that I would take with me into the field or down the road to the brook. It was my "car." This was during the depression and new tires were not available, so Dad would collect any that would fit the family car. There was a pile of unusable tires by the side of the garage. One Saturday I got the idea of looking for tires, too, to help Dad out. Dad was filing a saw up by the garage, facing the field that went down to the brook. I went to the brook and started following the bank upstream. About a half mile or so I found a large truck tire buried in the mud along the bank. I worked at that for about an hour until I could free it from the mud, stand it upright, and then roll it, mud and all, up through the field to the garage a half mile away.

I remember proudly presenting this big, mud-filled tire to Dad. He smiled and shook his head and told me that it was a truck tire, so it wouldn't fit his car. Years later, when we were reminiscing about the Ashland home, he told me he went and weighed that tire with a scale at the potato house where he worked, and it weighed 75 pounds! He said he recalled the incident well because what he saw was a strange sight. For a while, all he saw was a tire rolling uphill by itself. After a while he saw my head, a few inches shorter than the tire, as I struggled behind.

When the weather was good, some Saturdays Mom would let Buck, Dennis and me go to the neighboring Tilley farm a mile or so away and play with their kids and their animals. They had sheep that we liked to pet. One day I was ahead of my brothers coming from the farm back to our home when I heard a rifle shot at the house. Mom was by herself so I quickly ran to see what had happened. I ran to one of the back bedrooms and found Mom pulling in a 22 caliber rifle from an open window. She had just shot a crow that had been digging up and eating corn seeds in the garden she had planted a few days before.

As I think back of that time in my life, I was five years old, Dennis three plus and Buck was eight. As far back as I could remember, we were never restricted in our visits to neighbors some distance away. There was never a thought about abduction. We were expected to return by the next mealtime; as long as we did, there was no problem. Neighbors were all friendly and helped each other as needed. If Mom had had to restrain us and limit our movements, she would never have gotten the work done that was necessary each day.

How the world has changed during my lifetime. While I am on that subject, I want to bring up an incident that happened with our grandson, Jonathan, when he was about six years old. We had a cabin in Park Rapids, Minnesota, which we would go to off and on throughout the summer and fall. My wife, Pam, and Jonathan were there nearly every weekend. I would go whenever I could.

In 1989, Jacob Wetterling, an eleven year old boy from Minnesota, was abducted. This made national news and continued to be in the news off and on for many years. For Pam and I, and many parents in Minnesota, this was a turning point concerning our children and strangers.

Jonathan liked firetrucks. This one weekend, the Park Rapids Fire Department was giving kids rides on one of their firetrucks. We thought this would be great for Jonathan and he was excited to hear about it.

When the time came we got him on the firetruck with half-dozen or more kids and asked where the truck would drop off the kids. They said it would be at this same spot. Pam and I waited at the spot but no truck showed up. After waiting an extra five minutes or so, we walked around the corner and found that the truck had stopped in the middle of town and all the kids had already come off the truck. We didn't see Jonathan and began to panic, thinking the worse.

Pam confronted the firemen and asked why they didn't drop off the kids where they had picked them up. They said it was their last trip and decided to make the change, since the kids wouldn't have so far to walk. We got angry and said that our grandson was missing. The Mayor was there and Pam went to talk with him. I said that I was going to where we parked the car, in case he went there.

When I got to the car, Jonathan was there pacing back and forth in front of the locked car. What a relief, but our world had gotten darker and scarier.

Mom and Dad were both devout Catholics and would go to every church service that they could. There was a rural church in Frenchville, about three miles away, and a large church in Ashland, about the same distance. Dad made himself available to the priest, offering to help in any way he could. This was appreciated and used whenever there were season changes involving tasks he could perform, such as for Lent, Easter and Christmas. At one point in time Dad began preparing the church at Christmas time involving three decorated trees and a manger scene. Some Sundays we attended with Mom and Dad and other Sundays we didn't, depending on our health and other factors. Dad went to about every service. If we were having company for a Sunday dinner, Mom would opt to stay home with some of us younger kids and get the meal prepared. As a result, the importance of church going was instilled in us at an early age.

The year before we moved from Ashland, Buck got a female rabbit as a pet from a friend of his who was moving away. In a very short time this female surprised us all with a litter of rabbits. As the offspring multiplied, we began seeing more and more rabbits around our yard. One time we found a nest of newly-born rabbits. Dennis and I played with them. They were so tiny and cute. Mom didn't want any rabbits in the house so one night I sneaked one of the little ones to bed. Dennis and I played with it until we went to sleep. Next morning we found the rabbit flat as a pancake in bed. I had accidentally rolled over it during the night. We never did tell our parents about it.

Since I was five years old at the start of the school year, I was able to begin schooling. The school in Ashland was a single, 4-story building that housed all the classes through high school. There was no kindergarten at that school so I started in the first grade. As I said before, I was very strong for my age.

Buck was three years older than I and liked to tease other kids at school. It was not uncommon for him to come and find me when some kid was chasing him. I would take the kid down with a scissors lock across his waist and hold until he gave up and promised to leave Buck alone. I soon got a reputation for my strength. After that, when Buck would taunt someone, he would warn them that if they came after him he would get me. I wasn't a good fighter, nor did I like to fight. I used this technique several times and always had success.

Because of my strength, I could throw snowballs further than most people. And I was very accurate. I recall throwing snowballs at the large icicles that formed from the roof of the school building in the winter. And if there was a snowball fight, I was able to stand back beyond the range of other kids and still hit them with snowballs. One time I threw a snowball and hit a high school kid in the face. He was very angry and when he found out I had thrown the snowball, he came right up near me and threw one from close range. By anticipating his throw, I ducked and he missed. He got even angrier and threw another one, which I ducked. He was only a few feet away, but he couldn't hit me. The bell rang and he started toward the building. When he was some distance away, I yelled at him and threw a snowball. He turned and it hit him right in the face again. He was going to come after me but I had a couple more snowballs. He decided to forget it and went into the building.

One winter school day I was playing tag outside with several other kids during recess. There was a wood-fenced hockey rink to one side of the school driveway. It had snowed a few days before. The plows had piled the snow along the rink fence. The night before, it had rained and frozen. There was a layer of ice covering the snow bank. To avoid being tagged, I walked carefully along the icy snowbank. The kid chasing me was about to tag me so I made an extra leap, hit the ice and went sliding down the bank into the driveway and under the wheels of a moving Model A Ford.

The front and back passenger-side tires went across my chest. The driver was a high school kid who had been driving only a short time. I had the wind knocked out of me, but I wasn't hurt very much. In fact, I was very angry with this kid. I got up and proceeded to kick out his taillights. He got out of the car expecting me to be lying there. When he saw me get up and kick the lights, he fainted! They took him to the hospital for observation. I was rushed into the principal's office. The Principal and several teachers were there. They stripped me to the waist and saw the tire tread marks across my chest. They wanted to take me to the hospital, but I was too afraid and began screaming that I wanted to go home. Finally, they gave in and had someone drive me and my brother Dick home. My mother rubbed me down with rubbing alcohol and put me to bed. Next day I was back at school. Although I was not hurt by the accident, I did gradually lose my tremendous strength. I was still strong after that, but not to the degree I had been before. The teachers at school estimated that I had about 1500 pounds go across my chest, twice. *God's hand in my life.*

I remember the last day of school in Ashland. It was a warm, sunny day. They held a picnic outside in the schoolyard. We had coke to drink, sandwiches to eat, and after the sandwiches there were ice cream bars. It was hot that day and the ice cream bars were melting so they let us eat as many as we wanted. I ate three or four before they got too soggy to eat. That was my last day at the Ashland school because that summer we moved to Mars Hill, about 40 miles east of Ashland.

Growing Up (1941–1953)

MARS HILL

Mars Hill was predominantly an agricultural town, dependent heavily on potatoes. The Elementary School was located northeast of town and held all but the high school grades. The downtown portion of Mars Hill was one very wide north-south Main Street, with stores lining both sides of the street.

Figure 3. Mars Hill Main Street Looking North (Taken 2016)

Main Street continued south to the town of Blaine, a mile or so. Going north, Main Street ended at a curve to the right over a bridge. The bridge was just downstream from a dam that held back water from the Aroostook River. This formed a sizeable pond for fishing, swimming and skating. On the south-east corner of the pond was a starch factory where they would take low-quality potatoes and extract the starch from them. This factory has been long gone.

FIRST HOME

Across this bridge the road split into two side streets to the right, with the main road continuing north past the Elementary School. One of the streets on this side of the bridge was Pleasant Street. It was here where we moved to from Ashland. The house had electricity, central heating and indoor plumbing. It had been an Optometrist's home. One day Dennis and I went up into the attic and discovered cases of eyeglasses and lenses that had been left there.

Although the new house was a great improvement over the one in Ashland, it was not big enough for all of us. There was doubling up in the bedrooms, but no one had to sleep in the attic. There was an alcove along the stairway. Mom and Dad fit a crib in that area and that was my bed. I had to sleep in a fetal position to fit into the bed. I complained and my mother objected to my being in the crib; if anyone, it should be Dennis. Dad wouldn't hear of it.

One characteristic of Dad was that he preferred the youngest in the family. From the time that a member of the family was old enough to play with, he would only play with that one. In my case, I never remember him ever playing with me because Dennis came along 18 months later. By the time we moved to Mars Hill, Dad was taking Dennis with him on short trips. This affected me greatly, like I was inferior in some way. As a result I was very shy. If I wanted to ask something of Dad, I would usually go through Dennis, who had no idea why I wouldn't ask myself. As time went on I became distant with my Dad. Whenever he did take me somewhere by myself it was pretty quiet and a bit uncomfortable for the two of us.

I was close to my mother and would confide in her. She was a great help to me during this time with my self-esteem. I liked being with her and helped her with chores. I kept complaining about the bed and she kept telling Dad. Finally, they decided to have me sleep with my sister, Liz. She was around thirteen years old at the time and angry at having to give up her privacy. The arrangement was that I would go to bed around 8:30 p.m. or so, with the idea that I would be asleep when she came to bed. This worked okay except for one thing. If she got angry for some reason, she would dig her toenails into my legs. After one particular time when my leg had several deep scratches, Dad found another house that solved the sleeping problem.

I don't want to leave the impression that Liz was mean, she wasn't. We got along well, otherwise. When I was in high school and she was married and having children, I would visit her often. She enjoyed my company and I hers.

We had moved into our new home a couple months before school started. We played outside every day that the weather permitted. Usually Dennis and I played together but once in a while Buck would be with us. This one time we were in a pasture some distance away from our house when we came to an electric fence. Buck pulled a long piece of grass and laid it on the fence to see if it was working. He said it was and asked if we wanted to have a fun experience. He suggested that we pee on the wire. I decided not to do that but Dennis really had to go, so he peed and got the shock of his life. Buck thought that was funny but neither of us did.

When it came time to go to school, I was very nervous. Being quite shy, I didn't look forward to going. Buck, Dennis and I walked to school (about a mile from the house.) Because Mars Hill had Kindergarten, Dennis had to begin in that grade, putting him two years behind me in school. At recess time one of the guys in my class challenged me, the new guy, to a fight. I didn't want to, but he kept egging me on so I took him down and put a scissors lock on him with my legs until he gave up. I had no problem with him after that and, in time, we became friends.

Next door to our house was a garage to a house that was empty when we moved in. The house was for the minister of the church across the street. At this time there was no minister, though they were looking for one. Church services continued there while they were looking for a minister. I remember hearing the singing from the church on Sunday afternoons and at other times. The music seemed to captivate me and I would stop what I was doing and listen.

One Saturday after we started going to school, Buck found that the side door to the garage was unlocked and led Dennis and me there. The garage was empty except for some paint cans, rags and paint brushes in a corner. The garage door had a row of small windows across the top. The side door had a window made of four small windows.

After a while Buck decided to take some paint and brushes and paint all the windows. Dennis and I didn't want any part of it, so Buck opened a can of red paint and painted all the windows himself. He then took paint on a brush and started waving the brush so the paint would spray all over. Dennis and I said we had enough and began to leave. Buck started leaving as well, but as he was heading for the door, he threw the paintbrush through one of the garage door windows. The noise of breaking glass caused us to run as fast as we could back home.

The following Monday at school, the local police showed up and talked to the three of us separately about vandalism at our neighbor's garage. They didn't accuse us but wanted to know if we had seen anyone in the area over the weekend. We denied seeing anyone. At the end of the meeting, the police chief got us together and asked again about seeing anyone. Buck was quick to respond that it was probably some kids he didn't like. The chief chuckled and asked if he would like a job. The church had hired a new minister and they wanted the garage mess cleaned up. Buck quickly negotiated a price and agreed to get it cleaned up that evening, which he did.

The first year in Mars Hill was one of discovery. Dennis and I, and sometimes Buck, would walk the area. We were only a few miles from the bottom of Mars Hill Mountain, which rose out of the farmland to about 2000 feet. It sat on the U.S. and Canadian border. There's a metal plaque embedded in stone on the top of the mountain, with Canada on one side and the U.S. on the other. Today, the mountain has ski slopes and an array of giant windmills.

Figure 4. Mars Hill Mountain (Taken in 2016)

Some days our walks took us toward the mountain and other days in different directions. One day Dennis and I followed a dirt road to its end then continued into an area with bushes. We went for a while and were about to turn around when we came to a large area totally covered with raspberry bushes. It was still too early for raspberries, but we saw lots of them growing. We decided to come back in a few weeks and pick some. A few weeks later we returned to find branches hanging low with ripe raspberries. We filled up two pails in no time. We went there for several years and were never disappointed.

Like any small town, in Mars Hill there was not a whole lot for kids to do. If they weren't kept busy, kids tended to get into mischief. There was a gang of kids, maybe five or six, who thought it would be fun to kidnap someone and act tough. They targeted Buck, the new kid in town, who was about their age. One day they enticed him to their hideout, a "shack" made out of large pieces of cardboard nailed to vertical and horizontal wooden slats, at the end of a field a mile or so from our house.

Dennis and I happened to see the kids leading Buck away so we decided to follow. From their open doorway we could see what they were doing. Once they got Buck inside their "shack" they tied him up. There were Swastika signs and the name: Heil Hitler Gang over their doorway. We could hear them talking about torturing Buck unless he did what they wanted. We heard enough and ran all the way home. We told Mom, who told Dad. Dad asked us what we had heard and seen. He was visibly angry so asked us to show him the place, which we did. When he got there he asked the kids what they thought they were doing with his son. The strong and mighty gang scattered, some making new doorways through the walls. That was the last we ever heard of the Heil Hitler Gang.

This was the summer of 1941. With World War II in full swing, Nazi's were not a favored group of people for Americans. That fall when we picked potatoes we saw a group of men with military escort picking potatoes in a field near ours. We learned that these were German prisoners who were here in the U.S. to serve time through forced labor. We only saw them a few times; always at a distance. Many of the local people were disgruntled because the prisoners were better treated than they were. Prisoners had many items that were recently rationed or not available to us, such as butter, sugar, flour, chocolate bars and Coca Cola.

I remember that during the first year we moved to Mars Hill, Dad had a phonograph with a radio transmitter in it. To listen to a record, you tuned to a specific frequency on any nearby radio. One evening we were in the living room listening to records (I don't remember if everyone in the family was there) when a storm came up. During the storm a lightning bolt hit the electric pole and transformer outside our house, followed the wires in and came to the outlet where Dad had the phonograph plugged in. All the power was now off so the room was dark. I was sitting on the side of the room opposite that outlet. What came out of the outlet was a ball of bright light (ball lightning) that appeared to be rolling on top of the phonograph cord. It was going slow; perhaps 10 feet per minute, but every one of us were mesmerized by it and didn't move or say a word.

The ball started out about the size of a golf ball, or a little larger, and slowly shrank as it traveled. It gave off sounds like small electrical sparks and was bluish-white in color. It was moving toward me on the phonograph cord. About three feet or so from the outlet, the cord bent toward the phonograph. I didn't know what this thing was but I sure didn't like it coming in my direction. I hoped it would continue to follow the cord, but it didn't; instead it stayed on a direct course heading my way. It was rolling along the carpet getting smaller and smaller. About a foot or so in front of me it burned itself out, leaving only a small charred spot where it disappeared. After the electricity was restored, we searched the carpet and the cord for other burn areas but there were none. It was sure a scary experience, for me at least.

SECOND HOME

Life in Mars Hill was quite a change from what we were used to in Ashland. Our home had electricity, water, plumbing and propane gas for the kitchen stove. No more trekking out to the barn to visit the outhouse; or taking the long walk to the pump for water. We stayed in the first house about a year or two, and then moved to a much larger house at the north end of Main Street. It was this second house that I think of as my home as I was growing up.

The house had been a boarding house. Upstairs were five bedrooms, a bathroom and a small kitchen. On the main floor there was a bathroom, kitchen, dining room, living room, family room, pantry and a large playroom that had been added to the house. Then there was the large wood room, just off the playroom. There was an unfinished basement where there was a large furnace and shelving where Mom stored all the items she canned in the fall.

Figure 5. Second Home (Taken in 2016)

The house had two sets of stairways going up to the second floor; one off the living room, the other off the kitchen. The stairway going off the kitchen had very narrow steps, requiring care so as not to slip. One time Mom was going up the stairs carrying sheets to make the beds when she slipped and fell, tumbling all the way back down. She had a lot of bruises but no serious injuries. After that, she would take the other set of stairs even though it was a much longer walk.

I remember that there was a pantry beyond the stairs in the kitchen and there was an original GE refrigerator with the cooling coils in a cylindrical shape above the box. It wasn't big by today's standard, but it was a far cry from the older ice boxes where a block of ice was laid into the top so that as it melted, the cooler, heavier, air would keep the lower area reasonably cool. In those units, a block of ice would last three or four days, requiring constant replenishment during the summer.

The furnace was a huge monster of a wood-burner. Heat was distributed by insulated water pipes to registers throughout the house.

I remember my first impression of the furnace was like a giant octopus, its insulated-pipe tentacles coming out the top of the furnace, heading in all directions toward distant registers.

The house had a front porch with large white Roman columns. This porch came off the living room. There was a second, smaller porch, also at the front, but back a ways, that came off the kitchen. A third entry to the house was through the large playroom from the driveway; and a fourth entry came into the playroom from the enclosed wood room and walkway leading between the house and the garage.

Dad bought a full sized pool table and installed it in the playroom. This was a favorite pastime for Dad and company who would visit. The room had a wood stove in a corner and would easily heat up this large room even in the coldest of winter nights. Playing pool was also a favorite pastime for Dennis and I and our friends. It was a Godsend for us and our mother on those rainy days when we had to stay inside.

In the winter when we had friends over to play pool, Mom would get the stove going and she would make raw fried potatoes for everyone to munch on. She would peel potatoes; slice them into quarter-inch-thick slices, which she would place on a hot, dry skillet, cooking both sides of the potatoes until they were brown. The cooked potatoes were placed in a large bowl, butter was placed onto the hot potatoes and a little salt sprinkled on them as well. Everyone liked the potatoes. We would eat them with a fork while we played pool. Mom never minded cooking over the hot stove. Her satisfaction was watching the food disappear. I often thought my friends came over more for the food than for the pool playing.

By this time, Dick had graduated from high school and gone into the Navy. Dad would get wood logs hauled in. He and Buck would saw up the logs into blocks for splitting. Dennis and I split as best we could and would help bring in the split pieces to a room in the shed. In a typical winter we burned 10 to 15 cords of wood.

I remember one spring day Dad cut a very large poplar tree that was out by the main highway. The tree was probably 4 feet or so in diameter. The state was putting in a new, wider highway. The tree was too close to the new highway so it had to come down. Once Dad got the tree down and cut up, he put all the cut up wood blocks on the side of the house near the woodshed. It was Dennis and my job to get the blocks split and stacked by fall. It took us all summer to split up all the blocks of wood. Even then, there were pieces with knots that required Dad or someone else to split.

It was fascinating watching that new road go in. They dug out the old road. Widened it a few feet on each side, and then brought in various kinds of materials, layer upon layer until they got to the top layer which was crushed rock and asphalt.

We had a very large sugar maple tree, also near the road. It was a favorite tree of ours because it was so easy to climb. The tree was just into our property far enough so that it was spared when the road was widened. Dennis and I would climb the tree and virtually disappear from sight because of all the large leaves. It was also a good place for us to lay under on hot days, enjoying the cool shade.

The maple tree was probably 3 or so feet in diameter. One spring Dad decided to tap the tree for syrup. He placed several taps on the tree to collect sap. I recall Mom boiling sap for a couple weeks. When it was all said and done, from 45 gallons or so of sap we ended up with about one gallon of syrup. The syrup was the best I had ever tasted but Mom said the amount of work and heat that went into it wasn't worth it. Her feelings must have registered with Dad because they never made maple syrup again.

The maple tree was near our property line between us and our neighbors, the local banker, to the north. Near that property line Dad had put in horseshoe pits. Dad liked horseshoes and often played when there was company over. Dennis and I began playing horseshoes and eventually got very good at it. My technique was to throw a shoe so it would travel parallel to the ground and rotate. When I would do it correctly, the shoe would make one complete turn so the open end of the shoe was facing the metal stake. If I threw it perfectly, it would make a ringer.

Dennis is left handed and he threw shoes differently. His technique was to have the shoe rotate vertically. When he threw his perfectly, it would rotate so that the open end would come down facing the metal stake and he, too, would get a ringer. One summer we played so much and got so good that it was unusual if we did not get a ringer each time we threw. Many times we would have all four shoes as ringers. More than once we would be playing horseshoes into the evening darkness.

That big maple tree also produced a huge amount of leaves that needed to be raked in the fall. Raking wasn't much fun, but the huge pile of leaves from that one tree was always fun to play in. We exerted more effort in play than in work. We would rake the leaves into a pile then proceed to scatter the leaves as we jumped into the pile, getting totally buried in the process. Eventually we got the leaves raked and carried away, but not before their "play value" had been fully used up.

Dennis and I were not only brothers but best of friends as well. We had similar interests and enjoyed doing things together. Almost always, where one of us was, so was the other. In addition to the large maple tree in the front yard, there were several large trees in the back that we climbed as well.

We seemed to go through phases of outside interests. For a week or two we would play with whips made out of clothes line and a tree branch. One of our games was to take a tin can, set it on the ground and see if we could whip the can toward us. The way we played it, we would use our whips to measure distance to opposite sides away from the can. We would draw a circle on the ground at that distance. We would then stand on the circle line on opposite sides so that the whip would just reach to the other side of the can. Being opposite each other, and standing that distance away enabled us to whip simultaneously without ever hurting each other. Whichever one of us was the first to whip the can toward us past the line on the ground was the winner. Although our whips got tangled up a lot, neither of us ever got hurt, and we had loads of fun.

After a couple weeks of whips, we would go onto something else. Another of our favorite things to do was to make our own darts and throw them at the trees in the back yard. Our darts were made from several items. The shaft was from match sticks with the heads cut off. The feathers were playing cards cut to the right length and shape. The needles were large sewing needles which were inserted into one end of the shaft where we had made a hole. We then used twine to wrap around the needle and shaft. We glued the twine and needle as well as the feathers and set them out to dry. In a couple hours of time we could make half-dozen darts. Once the glue was dry we would play our games.

We pretended to be hunters stalking prey. We would walk around the back of the property and throw darts as we approached each tree. Dad had made a large swing with suspended ropes at each end that hung from tree branches above. The swing seat was a wooden plank about eight feet long. We sat at each end of the seat facing each other.

Once we got the swing moving back and forth (usually by standing and alternately applying force with our feet while holding onto the suspension ropes) we would sit, spread our legs apart and throw darts so they landed between our legs…not the brightest game we ever played.

I was never satisfied with having ordinary darts. One time I decided to make a giant dart. I made this from a Tinker Toy wood shaft, playing cards, a large darning needle, lots of twine and glue. This dart was nearly a foot in length and probably weighed about a pound. It was an impressive looking thing but not very practical. After one or two throws the force of impact caused the needle to shatter the wood shaft. But it was impressive, nevertheless. Like the whips, our interest in darts would fade after a couple weeks.

We played marbles, mostly in the spring. We both had a large collection of marbles. One thing we did was take a cigar box, cut a hole in the top just big enough for a marble to go through. We would get neighbor kids to see if they could drop a marble from the height of their waist into the hole in the box. For every marble they dropped into the hole we would give them two marbles in return. Every marble that missed the hole was ours. I practiced and practiced so that I could drop a marble in just about every time. Whenever kids would complain that it was impossible, I would drop three or four in a row to show how easy it was.

Other kids got the idea and made their own boxes. My reputation for being good at dropping marbles into the boxes became widespread so that none of the kids with the boxes would let me play. But there were always a lot of kids that would play mine so I always had a good supply of marbles.

In the winter, Dennis and I played outside as often as we could. If we weren't sliding, we were snowshoeing, or making snow houses. We both enjoyed snowshoeing and would take jaunts into the woods where our little camp was located. With a good layer of snow, the landscape seemed transformed into something new and very different from the way it looked without snow. It was fun to see the different animal tracks in the snow. There were plenty of rabbit and deer tracks at different places in the woods.

During the cold winters, the pond ice would get sixteen or more inches thick. When that happened, a team of people would cut up the ice into blocks which were stored in an ice house not too far away. The blocks would be laid down and then covered with sawdust to keep them from melting in the summer time. These were the blocks used in iceboxes as well as other purposes. Once refrigerators came out, the demand for ice blocks greatly diminished. A few years later harvesting ice blocks stopped all together. I remember going into the ice house one summer in late July. I dug around in the sawdust and found a block of ice still frozen after being there for several years.

When the pond ice got very thick, town trucks would plow a large area for skating. I remember skating but I was not very good at it. My ankles were not strong enough to keep the skates erect so I skated with skates at an angle. I would continue skating until the pain in my ankles got too severe.

At times when there was no skating going on, various townspeople, mostly in their late teens or early twenties would drive onto the ice and cause their vehicles to spin. The drivers had a lot of fun and spectators enjoyed it as well. Sometimes there would be no snow on the ice for several weeks. It made ideal skating conditions; however, at the northern end of the pond, the water flowed in from a stream. It was not unusual for this area to have running water most of the winter. The ice in this part of the pond was much thinner than the rest. Many times out-of-town people would venture too far and need rescuing.

Mom and Dad raised a couple of pigs behind the house. They were fed table scraps and grew to be large hogs, which were then slaughtered. Mom and Dad processed most parts of the hogs. They also kept a cow and a horse at the house. The garage had a room in the back with stalls where the cow and the horse were kept. There was a trap door in the floor so that animal dropping could be shoveled through the door to the ground below. The back, lower part of the garage was open so the manure could be carted away for use on the garden.

I remember the cow was a Jersey, with a pretty face and gentle disposition. It was usually Buck's chore to milk the cow. Buck was a great one for practical jokes and he never missed the opportunity of squirting Dennis and me with milk. We always had a cat or two around and he got a kick out of squirting them as well. The cow met all of our dairy product needs from milk to butter. I remember Mom churning butter and separating cream from milk. A byproduct of the butter making process was buttermilk, which I enjoyed as well. Whenever there was unused cream that turned sour, Mom would pour the cream on a biscuit and sprinkle sugar over it. It was delicious.

The horse was called "Two Tons" and was a very large workhorse that was used to drag out logs when there were wood cutting jobs. Dick and Buck could handle Two Tons but I never even tried. He just looked too big and ornery for me, so I kept my distance. Buck was fearless and used to ride him in the field behind our house. He got Liz to ride him one time and the horse bucked her off. She decided after that to keep her distance, too.

The summer that I was thirteen, Dad had gotten a contract for telephone poles. He was already busy with other work and got this contract for Buck, Dennis and I to earn money. Dick was in the Navy at that time. I had my eye on getting a red and white 28" Columbia bicycle with horn, lights and streamers. Dad said if I worked for the summer I would earn enough to buy the bike.

We worked all summer long. Buck would fell the trees; I would limb them and Dennis and I would peel the bark off. Once the log was peeled, Buck would hook up Two Ton to the log and haul it out to a field.

At the end of summer, I had a great anticipation of buying the bicycle that I wanted so badly. Unfortunately, when it came time to be paid, all I got was a $20 bill. Dad said that the car and other expenses ate up the rest. I was devastated. Everyone tried to console me but I was angry and hurt by the bad news.

My Uncle Pete heard about the problem and said if I worked with him the next summer in the woods, he would buy me the bike before we started the job. I liked that idea so the following summer, Uncle Pete shows up with the Columbia bike and I was highly motivated to go to work. There wasn't time for me to try out the bike because we needed to start cutting wood as soon as possible. As I rode out to the work site with my Uncle, I had visions of riding that brand spanking new bike. I could hardly wait for the first day to get over.

Uncle Pete was to fell the trees and I was to limb them. He borrowed Two-Ton from Dad to haul out the logs. Dad had sharpened an axe for me. You could cut paper with it, it was so sharp. As luck would have it, my very first swing of the axe hit the log in such a way that the axe bounced right back at me and cut my right leg across the kneecap. I remember looking down into the 2-inch-long gash and seeing all the way to the bone. Then the blood started to gush out. Dad had driven out to the site and was talking with Uncle Pete when I let out a yell.

They both came running, decided that I wasn't seriously injured and continued talking. Seeing the blood come out of my leg, I wasn't in agreement with their casual attitude, but kept quiet. Finally, Dad poured some creosote on the open wound and wrapped it. He took me home and there I sat all summer long with my leg propped up. Even though the doctor lived across the street and two houses down, I never saw the doctor. Dad didn't believe in seeing doctors except in emergencies and mine wasn't an emergency. I would sit out on the front porch and watch Buck and Dennis ride my new bike.

Although the big house must have been a lot of work for Mom to keep clean, I really liked it. The living room had a fireplace in it. It was so enjoyable to sit in front of the fireplace and just stare at the fire.

The garage had a loft above where hay was stored for the animals. It was another favorite place to play when the weather was inclement.

Between the neighbor to our south and our home, Dad planted a very large garden. Both he and Mom worked the garden and it always produced a bumper crop. Mom would can the excess food which we would enjoy all winter long. I remember she would pressure-cook vegetables in special metal cans without the lids. There were two sizes of cans and, in any particular batch, she could do either size, or mix the sizes. The metal sides of the cans flared out at the top. Once the contents were cooked, she would remove the cans and put them on a hand-operated can sealer. Mom would place lids onto each can. The sealer took one can at a time and its cover and would seal the cans air-tight by bending the flared tops inward over the cover. It was a clever device.

She also put up jars of fruits and berries. By the end of fall, our basement looked like a grocery store with cans and jars stacked all over.

St. Joseph's Catholic Church was the next building beyond our neighbor to the south. This is where we went to church. When I was about eight years old, Dennis, Buck and I began instructions at the church to become Altar Boys. We would meet once a week at the church with the priest. Things were going well during the first three sessions. On the fourth session, the priest said I was no longer wanted as an Altar Boy. I asked why and he said he had seen me out back playing the previous week instead of being with Dennis and Buck receiving the weekly lesson. I had no idea what he was talking about. His mind was closed to discussing the subject, so I never became an Altar Boy. I have thought a lot about this but have never been able to figure out what really happened at that time unless the Lord caused it to happen.

Not being an Altar Boy was okay with me. I wouldn't have to be in front of everybody performing Altar Boy duties. Dennis and Buck didn't seem to mind, though. I joined the Choir, which was located upstairs at the back of the church. My voice at that time was clear and strong. Many complimented me on having the voice of an "angel". As time went on I would sing solo parts because of my voice. I never had a problem because I wasn't performing in front of a group.

I continued in the Choir through High School. At Easter Service the priest would walk to the back of the church facing the closed doors while I stood on the other side. He would sing something in Latin and I would respond in Latin. This happened a half-dozen times or more during the service. I did this every year. When I was twelve my voice was changing and I had no control over it. I told the priest that I did not want to sing that year and why. He down-played it and insisted I perform as usual. This time I was silent and did not respond. He never asked me to perform again. As soon as my voice settled down, I was back singing in the choir, but with a lower voice.

A year or two after the "Alter Boy" incident, the priest had Buck, Dennis and me in a Catechism class, learning the basics of the Catholic religion. We had private lessons with the priest. The priest would teach a lesson, give us an assignment to study during the week, and then begin the next lesson with a quiz that covered the previous lesson. I answered every question correctly. At the end of the seven weeks, there was a final test, which I aced. I remember the priest giving me 99% and telling me that was because no one is perfect. Today when I think about it, it seems a trivial matter; but at that time it hurt me because I had worked so hard to get all the answers right. Since the priest was such a strong figure in our lives, I had that feeling, again, that something was wrong with me, thereby lowering my self-esteem.

One of our many jaunts took us to the town dump. It was a smelly place but a favorite of ours and many town kids. There was always the possibility of finding something useful that had been discarded. Buck and several other kids his age would go there with 22 rifles and shoot rats. This area was also a favorite place for hobos, who had a "jungle" not far from the dump. Their "jungle" consisted of several temporary shacks in somewhat of a circle with an open-pit campfire space in the center, where they cooked their meals.

Although hobos were looked down upon by society, these were, for the most-part, people who migrated to different parts of the country in accordance with weather and jobs and kept to themselves. They weren't looking for handouts and gladly worked for what they had. They would come into Northern Maine in the fall of the year because of the abundance of potato-harvesting jobs.

Most hobos were the victims of the depression. They were homeless, migrant workers who traveled by freight train and would come to areas of the country during times when work was available. Like the homeless of today, they were looked down upon by society. A small percentage caused trouble, like in any society. The majority, however, were peaceful, law-abiding people who kept primarily to themselves.

One hobo, in particular, was our favorite. His name was "Happy." He was a large, gentle man who cared for others and liked the visits from us and other kids. We didn't know much about Happy, just that he'd be in the area for a few weeks and then disappear for a year. He smoked a pipe and was always willing to share the little bit of food that he had. He said his travels took him to several other places, like Texas or Florida. Faraway places to us. His travel stories delighted us which made him content to have us as company.

He seemed to be an educated man and he liked to read books. I would bring him some of my books, which he would read carefully and, when he was done, would return them to me on one of my subsequent visits.

He and the other hobos traveled by freight train, grabbing an empty boxcar or riding with cattle. If discovered by the railroad workers, they would be put off wherever they were. They would walk along the railroad tracks to the next train stop where they would board another freight train. Of course, their journeys were adventures in themselves.

I remember several years after we met Happy. He had just come into town and found the "jungle" destroyed. Some of the town folk didn't like the idea of hobos in the area and had destroyed their little shacks. It was a cold day and Happy was concerned about a place to stay. We offered to have him come home with us, but he would have none of that. We told him about a little one-room shack that we had in the woods behind our place. It was a shack Dennis and I had discovered the second year in our big house. It had been someone's place of residence because it had a little wood stove, a bed, a table and a few old chairs. Dennis and I had used it as our "hideout" whenever we pretended to be cowboys. We had never used the stove, but it looked like it was okay.

Happy was delighted to hear about it. We took him there and he said it would do nicely. We even brought him some food from home when we visited him later that first day. He had the stove going and had made some coffee. He thanked us for the food, but said we shouldn't have done that. He said he would be fine.

Happy looked so much older this time. His hair was now all white. He seemed slower than he had been before. We checked on him every few days, but seldom found him in. One day when we visited, all his things were gone. We had hoped to see him before he left again, but we were too late. We never saw Happy again.

Two days before Christmas Break, the police were at the school again. This time they were there to finger print everyone. The federal government was creating a national finger print file and was getting prints from kids all over the nation. When it came time for them to take my prints, the person taking the prints couldn't find any print for my right index finger. He looked at my finger and there was no print there (because I had sucked my finger for years and, as a result, my fingerprints were no longer visible). Holding my finger up, the person doing my finger prints asked, in a loud voice, if I sucked my finger. Embarrassed, with other schoolkids present, I strongly denied sucking my finger.

That bothered me greatly. That night I prayed to God to help me stop sucking my finger. Next day at school, some of the kids that had been in the room when I was asked about sucking my finger, teased me, making things worse for me. I prayed again that night for God's help. I was also thankful that we were beginning our Christmas break. I hoped that the kids would forget about it by the time school resumed.

On Christmas day, after we opened presents and ate a traditional big meal, Dennis got a call from Rodney Milliard, Dick's youngest brother-in-law, who was at Dick's place. Rodney was in Dennis' grade in school and had gotten a Chemistry set for Christmas. He wanted Dennis and me to come over to do some experiments with him. It was cold and the ground was covered with a lot of snow, but it was only a few blocks from our home, so we walked over. Dick and his wife, Lorraine, greeted us and asked if we wanted anything to eat or drink. We declined. They said that Rodney was in the basement.

When we got to the basement, Rodney had already found an experiment he wanted to try. It was to make flash powder, like was used before flash bulbs to create a bright flash of light when taking pictures. The instructions said to measure out two compounds and mix them well. Rodney had found an old, discarded metal container that had been used to bake bread. It was ideal to hold the flash powder mix. Rodney wanted a big flash, so we tripled the amount of ingredients. With the container on the cement floor, he measured out and mixed the ingredients. He didn't want to light the mixture, I eagerly volunteered. The basement was cold so I had been wearing gloves. I took off my right glove to light the match. I tossed the lit match into the container, but nothing happened. I reached down to retrieve the match when a flash went off, burning my hand black.

I yelled and Dick came down to see what was going on. He brought me upstairs to the kitchen and had me run cold water on the hand while he called the doctor to see if he could help me. The doctor said to bring me to his home (just down the hill). The doctor looked at my hand, put a lot of Vaseline on it and then wrapped it in gauze. It was about 7p.m. and Dick wanted me to come back to his home with him for a while, which I did.

As soon as I got in the house, my hand started burning and throbbing. I went outside and the cold air made the hand feel better. I stayed out there for about an hour, slowly walking around the house. Dick came out and said to come in and if it hurt, he would unwrap it and put it in cold water. As soon as he unwrapped the bandages from the hand, the burning and throbbing disappeared. Dick took us home and explained to Mom and Dad what had happened.

Because my hand could not be touched, but had to hang when I slept, Mom had me stay in the parlor on the sofa. I slept with the wrapped, burnt hand dangling over the side of the sofa. It took two weeks to heal. When the wrapping was removed, there was no evidence of a burn, I no longer sucked my finger, and fingerprints were coming back to my index finger. *God had answered my prayer.*

I want to insert a note here: In Bible Study Fellowship, which I mention years later, someone said to be careful what you pray for, you might get it in a way you didn't expect. When I heard those words so many years later, I immediately thought of this hand incident.

Friday and Saturday nights were often spent with home-made music. Just about everyone in the family and many friends enjoyed getting together at our place because the big playroom could accommodate a large group of people. Everyone either played instruments or sang; many did both. We had music at our house nearly as soon as we moved in.

Dad would pick up instruments in his travels, and soon had a steel guitar, banjo, several acoustic guitars, button accordion, violin and several harmonicas (or mouth organs, as they were referred to.) It was not unusual for visiting musicians who were putting on local shows to borrow some of Dad's instruments. Mind, you, Dad didn't play more than a plain acoustic guitar but he provided instruments for everyone else in the family until they could get their own.

Having a variety of instruments gave the opportunity for Dick, Liz and Buck to learn to play some of them. Buck was very good with the guitar and never had much desire to learn other instruments other than harmonica. Liz played the guitar. Dick, on the other hand, was inclined to learn several. I never had much desire for the traditional country music instruments (I guess because everyone else was already playing them).

We had an old upright piano at the house. When I was 12 years old I began plunking on it and eventually learned to play some melodies. I didn't like the sound of the piano so I experimented and ended up putting thumbtacks into the felt hammers so the thumbtacks would strike the strings. This gave a much livelier and quicker sound; like a barroom piano you hear in some of the old western movies. This sound spurred me on more to practice and eventually I learned to play with the left hand playing basic chords and the right hand playing melody.

During the summer when I was 15, my best friend, Dick, took me out to his farm where they had a summer workhand who played the piano accordion. I had never heard such a beautiful instrument and couldn't get enough of his playing. I decided right then that I had to have an accordion.

I saved my earnings from summer jobs during my 15th and 16th year. During these two years I worked for the father of a classmate of mine who raised beef cattle. My job was to clean out the barn and help with other chores. One of those chores was loading bales of hay onto the bed of a large flatbed trailer that was hauled by a tractor. The bales weighed about ninety pounds. Once the trailer was full of bales, they would be brought to their large barn where they were hoisted up to a loft. I worked in the loft taking the bales from the hoist and stacking them. This became feed for the cattle during the winter months.

By the time the second summer was over, I had enough spare money saved to buy my accordion. I bought a baby grand. It was about ¾ of a full-size accordion, but had a full set of bass and piano keys. I must have driven my mother crazy as I practiced the accordion whenever I could. Eventually, I learned to play it pretty well.

Albert (Mom's brother) played violin. He visited us one year and I remember him getting up one morning about 6 a.m. and playing Ave Maria. I got up and went to the Living Room where he was playing. The music was so beautiful; I had tears in my eyes. Mom's Dad played the concertina. He lived in Montreal and toured Canada with Albert when Albert was young.

During the week that Albert stayed with us, a music professor, who played concert violin, heard that Albert played the violin and came over to our house. Albert only spoke French and the professor only spoke English, so Mom and I interpreted, as needed. The professor had all kinds of classical sheet music. In the conversation, the professor asked if Albert knew certain classical pieces. Through my Mom and me, Albert said for the professor to play one of his pieces. The professor started playing a short classical piece. Once he got through, Albert said to play again and he would play along. As they both played, the professor eventually stopped and listened to Albert playing. The music was so beautiful that the professor put away his violin and left.

It was not unusual for family and friends to get together and play into the early hours of the morning. Songs were country and folk, but music would extend to jigs, reels, polkas and a variety of other kinds of music. No one read a note of music. All playing was self-taught.

Dad formed a band consisting of himself, Dick, Buck and a fiddle player who worked for Dad. Once in a while Liz joined them. As a band, they played at the radio station in Presque Isle every Saturday at noontime for half an hour. Dad called the band The Aroostook Lumberjacks and used the show to advertise his lumberjack services. I had learned a new song that was popular at the time, "I Can't Begin

To Tell You" by Bing Crosby, and had sung it at the house whenever I heard it on the radio. Mom liked my singing and convinced Dad to have me sing the song on the radio. Dad agreed and wanted Dennis to sing a song also.

I remember the radio studio had a very small room, barely able to hold four people standing at one time, let alone instruments. Whenever an extra person was present, Dad would stand outside the door, to make room. Dad had announced that I was going to sing "I Can't Begin To Tell You." When it came time for me to sing, I got tongue tied and had trouble getting started. Buck was playing guitar and he would do a musical turnaround and bring the music back to the start. On the second turnaround Dad came into the studio and said, jokingly over the air, "You better begin to tell us or we'll run out of time!" After another turnaround, I finally got the song sang. Dennis sang "My Bonnie" without too much trouble. Because of my problems, we were never invited to sing again. I was just as happy.

During the Second World War, Dad contracted with the government to cut pulpwood. Paper was a critical item and there was plenty of work if one wanted to put in the labor. His contract called for 1000 cords of pulpwood a year. He hired a crew of people and they would work all winter long. Trees were felled, limbed and then hauled out to an open field where they were cut into 4-foot lengths and piled to 4-foot heights. A cord being 4 feet high by 4 feet wide by 8 feet long, a thousand cords would be a 4-foot-high stack of these logs, 8000 feet long. Whenever there were enough cords cut for several truckloads, they would be hauled out to the Great Northern paper mill in Millinocket, Maine. At one time this mill was the largest in the world. Dad visited many times and said that one of the buildings was about a mile long. This may have been an exaggeration but it was a long building.

Cutting pulp was hard work, but a lumberjack could earn a good living. Because there were scarcities during the war, most things were rationed. Tires were in limited supply so most people continued repairing their tires, since new ones were not available. Because Dad had a government contract, he enjoyed exemptions from the rationing so that he could buy tires or other items needed to get the pulpwood cut.

His favorite uncle was Uncle Nun (his Dad's brother). Dad had many stories about Uncle Nun. I always suspected that the stories were made up. One story I recall was when Dad took Uncle Nun with him to a government-run store in Houlton where Dad could get the things he needed for the pulp business. Uncle Nun had insisted he come along with Dad even though Dad was reluctant to take him. It was a long drive to Houlton to the government store, so Dad decided to take him this time. Uncle Nun seldom traveled. On the way to the store they passed a place that sold headstones. The front yard was covered with samples of their products. As Dad and Uncle Nun passed by, Uncle Nun did a double-take saying, "My God there are a lot of dead people there!"

When they got to the government store, Dad told Uncle Nun not to bother anyone; he could not buy anything there anyway. Dad said they would only be there a little while. When Dad had made his purchases he looked around and found Uncle Nun at a counter talking to a female clerk. He went over and heard his uncle ask a female clerk if she had taken a bath that day. Dad apologized to the flustered woman and asked Uncle Nun why he wanted to know. Uncle Nun said, "Well, I figure I've got to kiss someone's ass to get something here, and I wanted to be sure it was clean."

Dad was able to buy new tires at the store, but even so, they wore out faster than he could replace them. It was not unusual to have several blow-outs on a trip of 100 miles. When a blow-out occurred, everyone got out of the car. Dad would jack up the car, remove the tire, take out the inner tube, and, using a special kit made for that purpose, scrape around the hole to make it rough, patch the hole with special quick-drying glue and rubber patch, replace the tube in the tire, pump up the tire with a hand pump and remount the tire. On one 117-mile trip to Bangor, this happened 3 times down and twice back. This 234-mile round trip made for a long, long day.

When I was in high school, I was called by the priest to meet with him. It was a Saturday. When I got there he said that a high school girl wanted to become baptized as a Catholic but she had no one to be her Godfather. She had asked the priest to see if I would be her Godfather. He wouldn't tell me in advance who the girl was. He asked if I would be her Godfather, but added that if I did, I could never marry the girl. I asked again but he wouldn't tell me who she was. He said I could think about it and tell him after church the next day.

I prayed about it and felt honored that someone wanted me to be their Godfather. I decided to go ahead with it. In a private session in the evening that week, I discovered it was a girl a couple of grades behind me in school. I didn't know her that well, but was glad to help her out. An Aunt of hers, who was a regular at the church, became her Godmother. The girl thanked me several times afterward.

One late fall Saturday when I was fifteen years old, my best friend, Dick, asked if I wanted to camp out with him on the top of Mars Hill Mountain. I had never camped out before and thought it would be a lot of fun. He was an Eagle Scout and had a tent and necessary equipment. It was a nice day so we took our time climbing the mountain (about 2000 feet high). We set up the tent. He got some dry wood for a fire. We had taken sandwiches with us for today's meal, but we would build a fire in the morning and cook breakfast on the fire. We talked a lot that evening and then went to sleep.

Next morning it was foggy and drizzling. The wood was all wet, so we couldn't build a fire. It was about 40 degrees out and we were both shivering. I had only a light jacket. We decided to break camp and head back down the mountain. By the time I got home, I was coughing and had a fever. Mom had me undress down to my underwear. She had me lay in bed and removed my undershirt. She then made a mustard plaster with slices of onion in it and placed that directly on my chest and wrapped it with cheese cloth. I had developed pneumonia and was in bed three days. Each day she would make a new plaster. It smelled awful, but by the end of the third day, my fever broke. The next day I was up and around. *God's hand in my life.*

In the fall when I was sixteen, a high school friend asked if I wanted to go hunting with him and his Dad. We would be going out in a forest to the end of a logging road, about 8 or 9 miles. It was a good area for pheasant and deer. I agreed to go. When we got there, the three of us walked into the woods together toward a nearby lake. When we got to the southern end of the lake, we split up, agreeing to get back together at the car around noon for lunch. I had never been to this area before, but I had a good sense of direction and didn't worry about anything.

I walked in a given direction for a while, and then would retrace my steps to be sure I could find the car, which I did. I then headed back out and began hunting. I didn't see any deer, but I did get two partridges. It was past 11 a.m. so I headed back toward the car with rifle and two birds in hand.

Somehow I missed seeing the car and kept walking until I was getting into a swamp. I knew that was not right. The weather got worse; it began to drizzle and snowing a bit; all I had on was a light jacket. I backtracked, but could not find the clearing where the car was parked. Now I began to get concerned. I had visions of being stuck in the woods overnight, so I prayed, asking God to lead me back to the car. I kept walking for quite a while when I saw light glistening off water. It was the lake and I was just about to pass by the northern end of the lake. I walked around the lake to the southern end and, within a few minutes, found the car. *God's hand in my life.*

It was about 1 p.m. and my friend and his Dad had not returned to the car. I laid the two partridges on the floor of the car and began worrying about my friend and his Dad. I sat in the car and ate my lunch.

That afternoon, I went back to the lake in hopes of finding my friend and his Dad. I had no trouble finding the car, so I ventured out a ways further, but never saw them. It was beginning to get dark and much colder, so I went to the car and sat. Every once in a while I would shoot off my rifle in hopes of hearing a response from them, but never got a response. At midnight, my friend's uncle and aunt showed up. I was shivering really hard. They put me in their truck and turned on the heat. I explained what had happened. The uncle had a 32 rifle. He shot it three times, but never got a response. They took me home and formed a search party for the next day. Meanwhile I had gotten pneumonia and Mom did her mustard plaster thing again. Three days later I was cured, like before. *God's hand in my life.*

The rescue mission continued for a week, but they were never found. About 10 days later, my friend and his Dad walked out of the woods on their own and called for someone to come pick them up. They had found a cabin and were able to start a fire. They stayed in the vicinity of the cabin for a few days, and then they decided to head out, hoping to find someone. For the next two days, they would end up back at the cabin. Finally they changed their course and found their way out of the woods to a farmer's place, opposite from where they had left the car.

I dated when I was in High School. Although I didn't drive, a school mate of mine would ask me to get a date and we would go to a movie. I was so bashful; it was difficult for me to ask a girl for a date. I would finally ask and was never turned down. I didn't have a girlfriend, as such, but dated several girls.

I remember one date with a girl I really liked; when we got back to her house and I walked her to the door. We talked for a while. I wanted to give her a kiss but didn't have the nerve, so we kept talking. Finally, my buddy in the car with his date got tired of waiting and flashed the lights. I said goodnight to my date but never did kiss her. When I got home I was so angry at myself.

Although I did not have a steady girl in high school, I had acquired a reputation for being a "ladies man". According to rumor, I had several girlfriends. This came about because I would accompany different girls to their homes after school. I remember a new girl in school, a couple grades behind me. She was a blonde, beautiful and well endowed. One time I walked her home and the next day one of my female classmates confronted me, saying she knew why I was going with the blonde; it was because of her big breasts! I just smiled and felt good that someone thought that the blonde was my girlfriend.

One of the customs we had at the time happened on May 1st. A boy was to hang a May Basket on the door of a girl he liked. The boy would ring the bell or knock and begin to run away. The girl would come out, see the May Basket, and chase after the boy. If she caught him, she was to give him a kiss.

The baskets were a thing of art. My mother would make one each for Dennis and me. At the bottom of the basked, inside, was a sort of nest where you could put candy or a note. I would hang my basket, but I was so shy I never let a girl catch me, which kind of defeated the whole purpose. I guess I felt good that a girl was chasing me.

AFTER GRADUATION

After graduating from high school in 1952, I wasn't sure what I wanted to do with my life. I didn't like the idea of staying in Mars Hill, although I liked the town and the people. It seemed that my future would be limited if I stayed there. I wanted to get a good-paying job somewhere and do some traveling, as well. At the graduation ceremony, I gave the Address to the Undergraduates and said that they should seek a college degree to compete in the world. I took my own advice and went to the University of Maine for a year. I liked the lab experiments, but I couldn't see the application of basic topics like Physics or Chemistry. I wanted something practical I could do with my hands, instead, so I dropped out after one year.

I got a job as a plumber's assistant at $40 per week. I liked working with my hands and enjoyed learning the various tasks. A couple months later, my oldest brother, Dick, was running Al's Diner in downtown Mars Hill and looking for help. He approached me with an offer: if I would work at the restaurant for one year and wanted to stay on, he would train me to be a chef; if I didn't want to stay on, I could leave with no hard feelings. He would pay me $40 a week and my meals were free when I was working. I decided to work for Dick as a short-order cook. I made sandwiches, peeled potatoes, helped prepare some of the other menu items and, of course, washed the dishes. It was a good job.

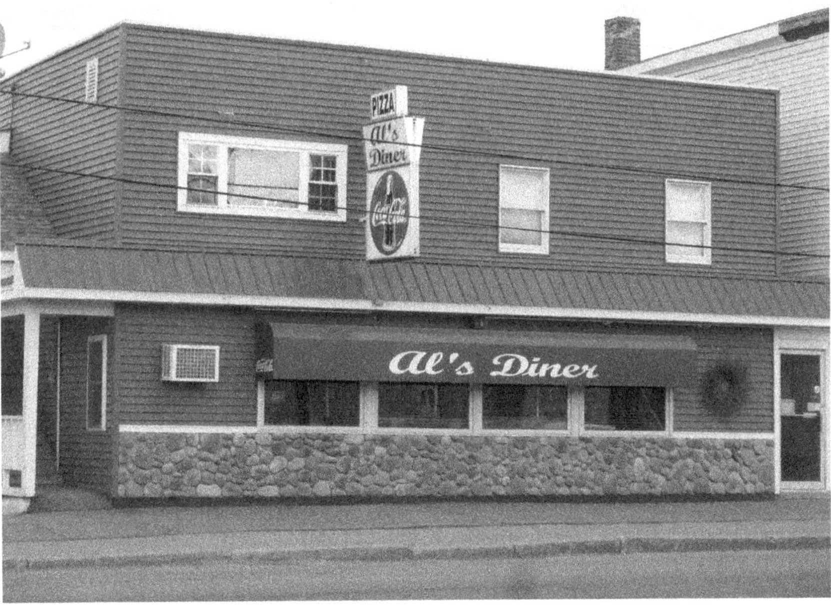

Figure 6. Al's Diner (Taken in 2016)

Dick was very patient and I learned a lot. There was one customer who would bring in items not on the menu and Dick would prepare them for him. One time he brought in sweetbread, in this case the testicles of a young bull. I was disgusted that Dick would prepare such a meal. He and I had a talk about it. He saw no problem with it and I wouldn't prepare anything that was not on the menu. As a result, at the end of the year, I told Dick I didn't want to stay on. As I look back, even this was a prodding by the Lord to move on.

I was now unemployed and no plans for the future. Dick, a friend of mine had graduated from high school. He would come over to play pool once in a while. We were good friends and he asked if I wanted to spend a week with him at his uncle's cabin. It was hunting season and we could do some of that as well.

It was a nice log cabin near a brook. It had a wood stove and several bunk beds. It was far enough in the woods that you seldom heard anything but nature's sounds. I brought one of my Dad's rifles and an old 22 pistol. That afternoon we went to the brook to try and catch some trout. Instead of trout, I caught a moray eel. I had never seen such a thing. Dick came over and told me not to touch it. I remember looking into the mouth of the eel and seeing rows and rows of teeth. Dick took out a hunting knife he had strapped to his hip. He had me drag the eel onto shore where he quickly decapitated it. After seeing the eel, I had no desire to continue fishing.

That night Dick and I talked a lot, reminiscing about high school and finally getting around to what we would be doing with our lives. He said he was going into the Air Force and was seeing the recruiter in Presque Isle the Monday after we got back. To join the Air Force, you had to sign up for four years. That seemed such a long time to me. He talked about the opportunities for learning any trade of your choice, including electronics. That caught my attention. Electronic Maintenance was a big emerging field. I told him I'd think about it.

Next day we went hunting deer. He knew of a field where deer were usually seen. It was a big field with woods at the far end. He said the deer would usually come out and eat some grass at the edge of the field. He had me lie down near a mound and keep an eye on the end of the field while he went a ways over where other deer had been seen.

I had never shot a deer; it would be quite an experience, and we could use the extra meat it would provide. All of a sudden out comes a 12-point buck. He looked all around before coming out further to get some taller grass. I laid the rifle on the mound, began sweating, was nervous and started to shake. I lined up the sights on the buck and then my eyes began tearing up and my heart was beating fast. I had heard of Buck Fever, but had passed it off as a hunter's tale. Here I was experiencing it firsthand.

The buck continued eating, looking up every so often. Meanwhile I was trying to stop my hands from shaking and getting more upset. Finally, I took a deep breath and began to calm down. I got the buck back in my sights when a noise scared him into the woods. My first and only time to shoot a buck and I was unable to do it. I stayed in the area the rest of the morning, but no more deer. We agreed to meet back at the cabin for lunch. Dick showed up a few minutes after I got there. He hadn't seen anything. I told him what happened and he laughed and teased a bit.

That night after we went to bed, we both heard a scratching sound out behind the cabin. Dick didn't want to go out because it could be a bear. I foolishly said I didn't care; we needed to know what was causing the scratching. We took a flashlight and my 22 pistol. The sound was coming from under a log toolshed. Because the ground under the shed sloped toward the back, the back of the shed was on stilts about a foot above the ground. We looked under the shed and there was a groundhog, scratching and gnawing at the shed floor.

I wanted to kill him with the 22 pistol but not under the shed. Dick got a long stick and prodded him out. The groundhog is a slow-moving animal so, to save bullets, we decided to hit it with large rocks. There was a pile of rocks nearby. We hammered the groundhog several times with good sized rocks, but with no success. Out of frustration, I shot him several times, but he continued to wobble around. Then I remembered what my Dad had said about groundhogs; that they were one of the few animals you could kill without a weapon, all you needed to do was hit them hard on the nose. Sure enough, one good tap on the nose and the groundhog was dead.

The rest of the week was without incident. We left for our homes on Saturday. I told Dick to stop by the house on Monday on his way to the recruiter and I would give him an answer. That weekend I talked it over with the family, and they all thought it would be a good thing to do, but it was my decision to make. That Monday I went with Dick to the recruiters and enlisted in the Air Force. A week or two later, a recruiter picked Dick and I up and took us to the train station in Presque Isle with tickets to Samson Air Force Base in upper-state New York. This was November 1954.

Military (1954-1959)

BASIC TRAINING

Dick and I got off the train and were bussed to Samson Air Force Base.[1] We, and about 30 other recruits, were assembled and immediately assigned to squadrons. Dick was assigned to a different squadron than I. We never saw each other again until a couple years later. When the last recruit was assigned a squadron, we marched to our barracks, were assigned bunks, dropped off everything but the clothes we were wearing, and then marched to the Quartermaster building to be issued military clothing. As we received each item of clothing, we took off the civilian counterpart and placed it in a duffle bag which had our last name stenciled on it. It began with shoes (brogans), socks, pants and belt. Spares of these we also placed in the duffle bag.

This was a large base providing basic training for several hundred recruits at any given time. The only two buildings I was familiar with at this time were my barracks and the Quartermaster building. As it turned out, we had to break for lunch and would finish the clothing process after lunch. Our Sergeant began marching us toward one of the dining halls, with us having civilian tops and military bottoms. Before we got started, I told the Sergeant that I had to pee pretty badly. He asked if I remembered the way back to the barracks, which I did. He told me my group would be at a certain dining hall and for me to catch up with them there.

I hurried back to the barracks, but the daily inspection had not occurred and the person on guard duty would not let me use the urinal or toilet. I told him I had to go really badly, but he refused and I wet my pants on the spot. Of course, the "accident" really showed through the khakis. It was at this time that a Lieutenant and his Aide came in to inspect the barracks. His Aide yelled "Atten…Hut!" The other recruit and I stood at attention. When the Lieutenant looked at me, he asked why I didn't solute an officer. I said, "I didn't know what an officer was." He looked at my clothes and asked how long I had been on the base. I told him this was my first day. His face relaxed and told us to be at ease. He then showed me the large eagle on his hat and the metal bar on his shoulders and told me that officers had the eagle and various metal insignias on their shoulders. He said any time I saw an officer, I was to salute him. I immediately saluted him, which brought a smile to his face. He told me to rejoin my squadron, so I headed back to where I had last seen them. By this time my pants had dried and the stain was not too noticeable.

I looked at the various buildings and couldn't remember which one the squadron would be in, so I headed to one of the nearby ones. As soon as I stepped inside, a Colonel, who was eating nearby, saw me and came to inquire. I saw the metal on his shoulders and saluted him. He saluted back then asked why I was there (it turned out this was the officer's dining hall). I told him my plight. He suggested I head back to the Quartermaster building and that my squadron would catch up with me there. Just as I left the building, I saw my squadron marching by. The sergeant saw me, halted the troops, and asked what took me so long. Rather than go into details I told him I had gotten lost. I am sure that the lieutenant and his staff, as well as the colonel, had an interesting tale to tell their friends that day. We finished getting the rest of our clothing and returned to the barracks. This was enough excitement for me for quite a while.

The last week of Basic Training we marched to a remote site. This would be bivouac training, which involved staying in pup tents for two nights. This was all part of survival training, but the weather was bitter cold and windy. Hot lunch included small boiled potatoes, meat and vegetables, and a hot liquid. We went through the serving line placing meal objects into our mess kits with gloved hands. The temperature at the time was 20 below zero with a 20 mile per hour wind. From the serving line we went to bar-height tables and stood to eat. In the five minutes it took for me to get served and find a place to eat, my boiled potatoes were cold. I swallowed the food as quickly as I could and dreaded the thought of bivouacking under these very cold conditions. I was starting to panic and beginning to think of going AWOL.

As soon as lunch was over, there was an announcement over the loudspeaker that bivouac was cancelled because of the bitter cold. We were bussed back to our regular barracks; Basic Training was nearly over. There were shouts of joy throughout the training facility. I heard later that 15 guys had frostbite as a result of the cold, which was the reason for cancellation.

We spent the next couple of days taking a variety of aptitude tests that would determine in what areas we were best qualified. My highest scores were in Electronics and Mechanics. I elected to be in Electronics and got my choice because of the high score. Next week we were given a seven-day furlough, with orders to report to our assigned base. Mine was Lowry AFB[2] outside of Denver, Colorado. I went home for a few days and then all the way to Denver by train.

MILITARY TRAINING

At Lowry, I was assigned to a training squadron with all the other recruits who were to receive training in Electronics. The training I received began with Basic Electronics, followed by Airborne Weapons Control Systems Maintenance (AWCSM). The training was comprehensive and very thorough. I liked it. Unlike college, here I could see a practical application of what I was learning.

Figure 7. Me at Lowry AFB (1955)

Once I completed the Basic Electronics portion of my training, I started the AWCSM training, at the Apprentice level. I was being trained to maintain airborne weapons systems for the F86, F89 and F94 fighters. The course was divided into several phases. I enjoyed the training and was doing well on my exams. Just as I was about to begin the last phase of training, I was pulled from the class and immediately began an Instructor Training course. There was a shortage of instructors and my grades had, apparently, caught the eyes of the training officers. I complained bitterly that I had not completed the maintenance course. They assured me that it was okay since I would not begin teaching that phase.

I was nervous about being an instructor, standing in front of a group of people. As with other types of training, the Instructor Training was excellent and, by the time I graduated, I had lost my fear of instructing a group. The training had instilled a confidence I had never had.

My very first instructing assignment was to teach the phase that I had not gone through (So much for assurances). I didn't know what I was going to do. This was the last phase of the course and these students would be going out to maintain this equipment. I prayed a lot about my situation.

On my first day of instructing, I had a class of fifteen men and began by announcing that I had been recruited for instructing and had not gone through this phase of the course. I told them I would work as hard as I could to give them the training they needed and deserved. Some of the people in the class were experienced maintenance technicians who had been maintaining older weapons control systems. They were career individuals who were motivated to learn the system. As soon as I made my announcement, the senior technicians said they would help as well. These technicians and I burned a lot of midnight oil preparing for each day's training. I would teach what I knew and they would jump in where I had difficulties. As it turned out, the technicians said it was one of the best training experiences they ever had. For me, it was the psychological boost that I needed to excel in teaching. In looking back, *I can see God's hand in all of this.*

The military had three levels of maintenance personnel: Apprentice, Mechanic and Technician. The course I started teaching was for Apprentice, or first-level mechanics. Upon graduation, an apprentice would be assigned to work with a mechanic who would show the apprentice the various tasks involved in maintaining the weapons control system. This included everything from where and how to obtain spare parts to disassembling weapons control systems components on the aircraft. Once the apprentice was able to function with little supervision, and had proven the ability to maintain the control systems, he would be recommended for upgrade to Mechanic level. This upgrade might happen in a few months or several years, depending on qualification of the individual and available slots for Mechanics. This process of advancement was similar throughout the various disciplines.

I did not have a driver's license. I received notice that a driver's training course was being offered for the first time at the base. I signed up. There were about a dozen of us in this first class. The vehicle we used was an old pickup truck that was difficult to get into third gear.

I studied the manual to learn all I could for each lesson. I had no vehicle to practice on except the pickup truck during class time. After twelve weeks of training, we all went downtown Denver to take our driving tests. The test course included driving on a one-way street and parallel parking. The first candidate from our class was a guy who did several things wrong, including going the wrong way on a one-way street.

When they got back to where we were, the tester told our instructor that he was not going to test any of us. He swore the guy he had just tested was trying to kill him. Our instructor apologized and pleaded with him. He asked to have one more tested and if that became a problem, he would leave with all his students.

The instructor picked me to be the next tested. I had done very well on the oral exam part and he felt confident that I could pass. I was nervous, but took the test. My only problem was trying to get the truck into third gear. There was a bit of grinding, but I succeeded. When we got back to the start, the tester was in a better mood. I passed the exam and he let others take the exam. The instructor only let those take the exam who he felt would pass. Five others passed the exam with me that day.

I attended church regularly at the base, but I was not into any Bible Studies. I felt obligated to go to Sunday Mass, but that was the end of my obligation. I was spending most of my time preparing lessons. I wanted to be as good of an instructor as I could be.

A friend instructor showed me a picture of his sister and suggested I write to her. He had mentioned me to her and she had told him that she would like for me to write. We started writing to each other for several months. She told me in a letter that her parents and she were coming from Ohio to visit her brother and was looking forward to visiting me. Her parents wanted to take my friend and me out to dinner. When the day came for me to meet them, I was too nervous and disappeared. Later, my friend asked what happened and I made up some story. That ended that relationship.

Advancement for me in the training discipline required learning to teach at the more in-depth levels. It meant I would begin teaching at the Apprentice level, and then advance to teach the Mechanic level, and, finally, at the Technician level. After a year or so of Apprentice-level teaching, I advanced to Mechanic level, along with a promotion. Another year later I was advanced to teaching Technician level, with another promotion.

Technician level went into design as well as function. These technicians would become the resident experts at whatever airbase they were assigned. Because of their expertise, they would be called upon to solve problems that were beyond the capability of the Mechanic. Every technician had several years of Mechanic experience, usually on several different weapons systems. Some were already at the Technician level, but were adding this weapons control system to their line of experience, either because their system was obsolete and being phased out, or they volunteered to advance to a newer system.

Because of the progressive experiences I got, I became knowledgeable to a far greater depth than if I had remained teaching at a lower level. This placed me as a candidate, along with a dozen others, to go to a factory school at Hughes Aircraft in California to learn the latest weapons control system; it would be for the F15. The assignment was to learn the new system well enough to then come back to Lowry and develop the training courses to maintain the system. I wanted to get this opportunity, but to do so I had to have 18 months left in the military after returning. As it turned out, I had to extend my enlistment by 6 months, which I gladly did. It's interesting when I think back to before I went into the military, I thought that four years of service was a long time; now I was glad to extend in order to get the additional experience.

During the six months of training at Hughes, I stayed at a motel with kitchen facility within walking distance of the Hughes Aircraft facility. Hughes training personnel wanted to see how effective their training was, so they had all of us take a pretest before training started. At the end of training they would give us a posttest to measure the difference, showing the progress provided by the training: the greater the progress, the more effective the training.

Although I had acquired a driver's license, I had no car. The training duty at Hughes was a good opportunity for me to save money, since the per diem took care of most of my costs. Within four months I had enough money saved to get me a car. I bought a 1954 green Ford coupe. I was so proud of that car.

I wanted to show off the car, so I invited a couple friends to go for a ride with me. Since my only driving experience was during the driver's training course at Lowry some time before, I had difficulty with traffic lights. My friends and I were going along a four-lane highway with little Sunday afternoon traffic. As I approached the lights, they began to turn from green to yellow. Although I was several hundred feet from the intersection, I pressed the brakes hard, causing them to squeal to a stop, still a long way from the intersection. After a bit of silence, one of my friends said: "You've got some good brakes there." That broke the ice. I apologized for having a heavy foot and everyone relaxed after that. By the time I left California, I was driving pretty well.

At the end of factory training, my final scores for classroom and repair were 100 and 99 respectively. This was the highest they had ever seen at Hughes. I, again, claim this to be *the Lord's workings*. I was told by the Hughes training manager that my pretest and posttest had predicted for me to do well, but they didn't expect this kind of result.

After getting back to Lowry, I was going to take a vacation and drive all the way to Maine when I heard from Dick, my buddy with whom I had joined the Air Force. He was hitchhiking from California, going to Maine. I told him if he could get to Colorado by the time I was to leave; I'd give him a ride all the way. He got to the base in time so the two of us started for Maine, taking turns driving and sleeping in the car. It was great seeing Dick again. It was helpful to me having another driver and he didn't have to worry about thumbing a ride the rest of the way.

After our vacations, Dick wanted a ride back to Colorado. He had to be in California a few days after I had to be back at the base, so it worked out very well for the two of us. We took turns driving and sleeping. I had my accordion, a big reel to reel tape recorder, a five gallon can of gasoline, and other items in the trunk. There were suitcases and boxes on the back seat and his duffle bag on the floor. Every time I drove, Dick would sit in the passenger seat or lay on the boxes in the back seat to sleep. We always switched off taking turns driving.

This one time it was about 11p.m. when we found a small town, St. Francis, on the border of Kansas and Colorado. It had a restaurant that was still open, so we stopped for coffee and a bite to eat. I had been driving and wanted to stretch for a bit. When we came out of the restaurant, I felt invigorated and decided to keep driving. Dick was tired and decided to sleep on the boxes in the back seat.

When we crossed into Colorado, the road was under construction. There were a few flakes of snow coming down and a cool breeze. As soon as I started into the construction area, all I saw was gray. Gravel was all over the road and no lines to mark the road center or edges. Within a few minutes I started falling asleep. I caught myself going across the road on the opposite side. My reaction was to pull the wheel back onto the road. I pulled too far and too fast, causing the car to slide sideways on the gravel highway. The car tumbled, first hitting the driver's side, going airborne and then hitting the passenger rain guard above the window and finally landing back on all fours.

Suddenly I felt a cold breeze hit my face and heard a voice from the back seat saying: "What the Hell?" The car was crossways in the highway. The windshield had popped out. We got out and looked carefully at the car. The driver's side window had a web-shaped crack where my head hit as the car spun around. The passenger's door and window were damaged where the car landed after it spun airborne for half a turn. I had received a slight scratch on my right side from gravel that had been scooped from the passenger's window opening which became deposited onto the front seat.

When I got a look at the inside of the car, I saw the steering wheel bent inward at the two places I had had my hands. I tried starting the car but it wouldn't start.

Figure 8. Carlton's Ford Car After Accident

It became a terrible realization that the only two places in the car where the two of us could have survived with minimal injuries were where we had been. If Dick had been in his usual place in the front seat, his head would have been crushed. *God's hand in my life, and, in this case, in Dick's as well.*

After a half hour or so, a bus from Denver was heading to Kansas and the driver offered us a ride to the town we had just left. I had to be at Lowry the next day and Dick needed to continue his trip westward. I told the bus driver I had to continue onto Denver. He said that there was a gas station in St. Francis that had a wrecker. He said the car had to be moved or the road crew would just shove it into the ditch. He would see if they could send out a wrecker and bring the car there. I told the driver to tell the mechanic that

I would be back to settle in a couple of weeks. The driver suggested I try and get the car out of the middle of the road, to the side.

I knew I couldn't start the car but I might be able to budge it using the starter motor with the engine in low gear. After several budges, I had the car at the edge of the road. After another 45 minutes, there was a car heading toward Denver. Two old men were in the car, having had a few drinks and going slow. We asked if they would take us to Denver. They wanted to know how much we could pay. Since it was about 110 mile to go and there wouldn't be many gas stations open, I offered to give them my five-gallon can of gas for the ride. They liked that idea. We took all of Dick's stuff out of the car and the gas can from the trunk. I placed everything I was not able to take with me in the trunk of my car and locked it. It was the only area of the car that was not damaged.

After the two men poured the gasoline from my can into their car, we all climbed into the car and headed toward Denver, at about 40 miles per hour. About a half hour later we saw an all-night diner and decided to stop for a pit stop and some coffee. I wanted to call the police to report the accident. The waitress said there was a pay phone by the garage, but it may not be working this time of night. I went down and tried, but no connection could be made. As I was walking back toward the restaurant, I felt a cold breeze down my legs. I looked down and found that my pants had split along the crotch, leaving the two pant legs hanging by my belt. I got a pair of pants from my suitcase and changed in the restroom.

When I caught up with Dick, he was at the counter, having ordered coffee. When I approached him his hand was shaking terribly and instead of sugar, he was pouring catchup in the coffee. It was just starting to hit him. We both got coffees and began to talk about what had happened.

I had the driver drop Dick off at the bus station in Denver and then arrived at Lowry around 6 a.m. that morning. I got my stuff out of the car and thanked the two men, who were still in pretty good spirits. Two weeks later, a friend of mine agreed to take me to settle about my car. When we got there, we found the gas station and behind it was my car. I opened up the trunk and everything was there, untouched. This included an expensive reel-to-reel tape recorder, my accordion, reels of tape, a radio and various other items. The car was totaled so I settled with the gas station owner to sell the car as junk. *It was obvious to me that the Lord had been with us during this accident.*

I saved up my money and in a few months bought a used maroon Lincoln. It was a heavy car and I could get around in the winter without snow tires, but it was a gas guzzler.

At this time I rented a near-by apartment off base. I was still very shy when it came to meeting girls. The owner of the apartment had two daughters, twins, in their late teens. She kept trying to get me to date either daughter, but I never had the nerve to do so; besides, I didn't know which one I would date. The girls' mother kept trying to push me on her daughters, making me uncomfortable. I moved to another apartment.

The secretary to my commander was a lady in her fifties; a strong Catholic. She and I got to know each other well. She had a granddaughter in her late teens. She showed me pictures of her. She wanted me to date her but I kept putting it off. Finally I agreed to take her to a movie. The movie "West Side Story" was in the theaters for the first time, so we were going to go. When we got to the theater, the lines were a block long and growing. I told her that the lines were too long, so we drove around for a while, and then I brought her home. I apologized when I dropped her off, but she ran to her house without saying a word.

When I went to work the next Monday, the secretary asked what happened. I told her about the long line at the theater. She said her granddaughter was so disappointed. That was the end of that relationship.

At Lowry, I was developing the Mechanic level training program and assisted on the Technician level as I was requested. I liked all this experience, but I was not pleased with the way promotions occurred. It had little to do with one's performance and more to do with time in grade. I was a Staff Sergeant at this time. I personally had no complaints about my promotions; reaching Staff Sergeant during first tour of duty was quite rare. My problem was the system. There was little incentive to do well, and I saw many examples of very capable people being made to wait because a less capable person with more time in grade got the promotion.

My commander came to me as my tour of duty was drawing to a close and expressed the fact that he really wanted me to stay on. I told him my problem and he offered me a promotion to Technical Sergeant if I would stay. I wasn't sure what I was going to do after leaving the military, but I wanted to explore what was out there.

Martin-Marietta (1959-1962)

TITAN MISSILE TRAINING DEVELOPMENT

When I left the Air Force, I was given a 90-day period of time during which I could come back with full reinstatement, promotion to Technical Sergeant and I would receive a $1000.00 reenlistment bonus. I told them I would think about it. I sent out a lot of resumes and answered many employment ads, but was getting no results. I was running out of money and was beginning to get desperate. Two weeks before the 90 days were up, I received a visit from a couple of guys from the base. They let me know that I could come back and get all the benefits they had promised. I told them I wanted another week to decide. They said they'd be back the following Friday. Tuesday of that week I got a call from the Martin-Marietta Corporation[3], on the outskirts of Denver, who was looking for people with skills to develop and teach maintenance training programs. They were building the Titan Missile for the military. I applied and was informed Thursday of that week that I had a job...one day before I would have gone back into the Air Force. *Coincidence? I don't think so.*

After receiving an orientation on the Titan Missile Program, all New-Hires were assigned different components of the system. There was the Fuel System, the Electrical System, the Mechanical System, etc. The system that tied all the other systems together was the Central Control System to which I was assigned. To understand how the Central Control System worked, I had to understand how all the other systems operated, as well. I liked that idea, since it forced me to learn the entire missile complex.

As soon as I could afford it, I moved to renting a two bedroom house in the suburbs of Denver with another person working at Martin-

Marietta, who I will call Jack. Jack was from Texas, with a slow southern drawl; a funny guy who was smart, but so uncoordinated. We got along well together, sharing expenses and chores. Jack worked in a different system from me. We would have lunches together on weekends, but seldom saw each other at work. He had his car and I had mine, and except if either of us were having maintenance done on our car, we drove separately.

One time it had rained and froze the night before. This particular day, we were heading out together to our cars. There was a spot of ice on the sidewalk, which I avoided. Jack came out and without looking, hit the ice and went head over heels. I made sure he was okay; he was more embarrassed than hurt. I said I'd wait, but he insisted I go on. He would change his suit and head on in.

I could see Jack's work station from where I sat. I noticed he didn't show up after fifteen minutes. I'd check on him every once in a while. About 45 minutes later, he gets to his cubicle, but didn't look around like he usually did. At break time I went over to see him and he was trying his best to avoid me, shuffling papers and opening drawers. After pestering him for a bit, he finally opened up. He said, "You know that ice spot I hit while you were there?" I said, "Yes, What happened?" He said that after changing his suit he proceeded to come out of the house and hit the same spot, taking another tumble. I had all I could do to hold my laugh; then he started laughing and so did I.

I was working with a civilian employee at the base. We were going to the same church and became good friends. I had dinner at his place a few times. One of those times I met his wife's sister, who I will call Jackie. She was a couple years older than me, divorced, had two kids and liked to ski. She was staying with her mother, who I met. As time went on I spent more time at the mother's place and began dating Jackie.

Jackie was fun-loving, liked drinking and would be what was called a "fast girl." Her sister objected to Jackie dating me, out of respect for me, not her sister. But Jackie did what she wanted to do.

One Saturday she invited me and my co-worker Jack to go skiing. This would be a new experience for Jack and me. Jackie assured us that the place she went to provided a beginner's slope, basic instructions and rental of all the gear needed. She said it would be fun.

When we got there, Jackie took us to the rental shop where we got all the items we needed. The rental included instructions for beginners.

They showed us how to "snow plow" with the skies so you would keep from going too fast. They also demonstrated going at an angle to the left and to the right as we went down the slope. They showed how to fall and the use of your third ski (your butt). Their greatest caution was to not speed, but go down the slope gradually, as they had demonstrated. Once we got ready for the beginner's slope, Jackie said goodbye. She was going to the advanced area and would see us at the bar later that afternoon.

Jack and I took the lift to the top of the slope. We were both a bit excited at trying this out. Although the slope was nowhere near as high as the more advanced slopes, it seemed plenty high to us. I started down first, doing a snow plow and angling to my left, then to my right. I was able to maintain a nice slow speed. About a minute or two after I got started, I saw Jack coming straight down the slope. As he was passing me he looked over, lost his balance and went head over heels. I made my way over to him. He was shook up a bit but said he was fine. I reminded him that we were to snow plow and go down at an angle. He reluctantly agreed by saying, "Yeah, yeah" and waving me away with his hands.

I started down the slope again. After a minute or so, here comes Jack again and took another spill. I was going to see if he was okay when he raised his hands and fended me off. I figured it wouldn't do any good to warn him again. I stood where I was at and watched him get up, head straight down the slope and fall again.

I shook my head and resumed my slow descent. By the time I got to the bottom, Jack was waiting. He had fallen a couple more times on the way down. He said he was giving up skiing and would meet me in the bar. I went back up the slope several more times and enjoyed it. We all met at the bar, had a drink and then headed to a restaurant Jackie knew about. Jack laughed about his experience.

The restaurant was in a bar, a popular place apparently. After a while I needed to go to the restroom. With a bit of a smile on her face, Jackie suggested that I look at the painting on the wall while I was in there. As I was coming out of the restroom, I noticed a painting of Adam and Eve in the Garden of Eden. They were both naked but their private parts were covered by a large leaf. There was a hand-written sign to not lift the leaf. (The leaf was made of metal and obviously placed where it would entice the viewer to ignore the sign.) Curious to see what was really under the leaf; I lifted it a bit, this triggered an alarm that sounded loudly throughout the restaurant. I realized now that everyone familiar with the restaurant knew what I did and would be looking at me when I went out of the restroom. I waited a while hoping someone would come into the restroom, but no one did. After five minutes or so of waiting, I returned to my table. Jackie had told Jack what had happened, so they both teased me, and, of course, everyone else in the restaurant looked at me with smiles on their faces; some even jokingly pointed a finger.

Jackie and I went on a few more dates but our personalities were so obviously different that we quit seeing each other. Her sister was happy about it.

One of the people hired to develop a training program was a young auburn-haired woman. Off and on I would write poetry. She read some of it and liked it. She was of the Jewish faith and we talked about religion and began liking each other. One day I got the nerve up to ask her for a date to a local restaurant. She insisted that she pay for her own meal. My instant reaction was to ask, "Do You think I'm a Jew?"

She said, "No, but I am!" and walked away from me. No amount of apology helped. I don't know why I said that. It is something I have never said before or since. It just blurted out of my mouth; but once the damage was done, there was no way to reconcile it.

At this point, the reader may be seeing a pattern with me and women. I liked them. I liked them a lot. I thought that they were God's greatest creation. But whenever I became interested in a woman something happened to end the relationship. This pattern continues until I meet Pamela in 1963. Looking back over my life, I think God was using my shyness or different situations to end relationships and have me wait for the person He chose for me. The reader may think this is farfetched; however, the changes in my work locations were also part of getting Pamela and I to meet.

At this time in my life I began feeling a thirst for information about Jesus, God, and a host of other topics. I had never read the Bible, so I bought a Catholic Bible and began reading it like a book. I began to see things in the Bible that didn't seem to align with my understanding of Catholicism. It also bothered me that none of the Catholic churches that I went to ever pushed Bible Study. In fact, Bible Study was never mentioned. This was not a big issue at this time with me, but it was something that began gnawing at me.

My military training prepared me well for this Titan Missile assignment. We were developing training courses to be given to military instructors who would in turn teach missile maintenance from our courses; a Train-The-Trainer program. We had a year to develop the courses after which time we would go to Wichita Falls, Texas, and present the courses to military instructors who would then continue the training to the actual maintenance personnel.

There was an arms race going on with Russia at this time, and Russia was ahead. The Air Force had built the Atlas missile, but was moving to the Titan missile in an attempt to catch up to the Russians. Normal time required to catch up to the Russians was estimated to be upwards of ten years. The military couldn't wait that long, so they implemented a Concurrent Development process to reduce the time for the U.S. to catch up.

In a normal development process, a product is built to completion before beginning to build its successor. In a Concurrent Development process, the second generation begins while the first generation is still being built, and so the third generation begins before the second is completed, etc. The idea is to begin the next generation as soon as there has been enough learned from the previous generation to improve the later generation. The concurrent process was very expensive and wasteful, but necessary to reduce the overall time by a significant factor. In this case, it reduced the time to catch up to the Russians to five years.

I began working on the Titan I Central Control System. Improvements garnered from the Atlas program as well as technical advancements were integrated into this training program. One of the advancements that had just come out was the use of transistors in place of vacuum tubes and mechanical switches and relays. The military had adopted Logic Diagrams to replace Wiring Diagrams for maintenance purposes. This forced us to learn a new way of looking at electronic circuits, and a new way of teaching their maintenance. This greatly simplified the maintenance task, once learned.

A normal work week was from Monday 8:00 a.m. to Friday 5:00 p.m. There would be an occasional Saturday meeting. Because everything I worked on was Secret, I couldn't take work home, freeing up my weekends. I spent a lot of weekends exploring the Denver area, going to movies and restaurants. I was earning good money and was able to save from each paycheck. After a year or so, I bought an American Motors Station Wagon, which served me very well.

My sister Liz and I corresponded with each other. She was divorced at this time and trying to raise six kids. Her ex-husband was an alcoholic and unable to provide her with any support. I had excess money so I told her I would send her $100 a month to help her out. She told me not to do that, but I insisted and so I did this for the next couple years, until she remarried and no longer needed assistance. She was always grateful for the money and thanked me many times.

I liked Denver and the area. I enjoyed traveling up into the mountains and exploring the various sites the state had to offer. Many of my weekends were spent visiting various places. One time in July, some friends invited me to come with them to go to a glacier. I didn't know there were any in Colorado, but after a two-hour ride and another hour of walking, we came to an area where there was snow on the side of a mountain. It wasn't huge, probably several hundred feet up the mountain by about 50 or so feet wide. The snow was melting so that cold, clear water was running from the bottom of the glacier. The snow on top of the glacier was slushy and made for good sliding. Each of us had our try at sliding on our feet by climbing up along the edge of the glacier a ways and then getting on the snow and slide standing up, as best we could. It was a lot of fun and hard to believe that we were doing this in July. The outside temperature here was probably 50 degrees or more.

One weekend I went to Colorado Springs, taking in The Garden of The Gods and other sites. These escapes helped me to forget about work for a while. I enjoyed my work, but it was very intensive and these escapes helped me relax.

Another way I relaxed was playing my accordion. It had survived the car accident while in the military, with a few scratches, but it played well. Music, for me was an escape, once I started playing, my concerns melted away.

Work on the Titan Missile progressed fairly well, with one major setback. Because development was concurrent, about halfway through the training development for the Titan I, we had to switch over to the Titan II. This involved learning the differences between the two systems and changing only the portions of our courses where changes occurred. There was a lot of griping and, it seemed to us, such a waste of time and resources. We were reminded that it was a necessity in order to catch up to the Russian missile program. No more gripes after that. In fact, things seemed to go faster because we all realized this was a race, after all.

Once the courses were completed, we and our courses were sent off to Wichita Falls, Texas, where we began training military instructors who would then do the training for the military.

WICHITA FALLS

When I got to Wichita Falls, Texas, I stayed in a motel until I found more permanent quarters. Not far from the motel was a music store. That Saturday I went into the store and discovered that Hammond had recently come out with a Chord Organ, really an electronic accordion, with base keys on the left and regular piano keys on the right. It was laid out like an accordion except you sat down to play it like a piano. I started playing it and found I had no trouble, except for locating some of the base keys. I was so impressed, I asked if they could deliver it to my motel, which they did. I really liked the organ and when I rented a house for my duration, the Chord Organ went with me.

A friend from work and I shared a two bedroom house. It was furnished so all we had to do was move in. I even got the music store to move my organ. I would go to the store quite a bit and play for them, demonstrating the chord organ.

The military training went off like clockwork. The instructors were experienced trainers and learned the new courses quite easily. It was a fun assignment. The instructors were familiar with Wichita Falls and would take some of the guys to a bar every Friday night to have beer and pizza, and watch gals do a strip tease. They kept asking me to join them to have a pizza (they never mentioned the strip tease). I had never had pizza, so after several weeks of their pleadings I joined them at the bar. I couldn't believe what I saw. These guys were gobbling down pieces of pizza with grease dripping from their chins, and saying how good it was. I didn't like it at all. I was about to leave when they grabbed my arm and said "Wait, the best is yet to come." Just then a young woman with tassels on her nipples and only wearing a G-string came out and started dancing on a stage. I had never seen anything like this. As she danced, she twirled the tassels and all at once, one tassel came off. In embarrassment, she cupped her hand over her breast and ran off stage. I had seen enough and left.

My buddy (who I lived with) and I made friends with a neighbor who lived behind our house. He and his wife invited us over to dinner, and we had them over as well. They heard that I played music and asked me to play something, which I did. We all sang songs and had a great time. Next Friday evening, my friend from work invited friends to come and listen to the music and dance. Before long, we had a houseful of people on Friday nights. It was a lot of fun until I found some guys making out with girls in the bedrooms and called a halt to the Friday night music.

A few weeks after arriving in Wichita Falls, one of the military instructors had a sister (I'll call Sarah) living in the city who was looking for a male companion. The instructor had mentioned me to her. He asked if I would like to call her up to make contact, and we could go from there. After hearing more about her, I decided to call her up. He told her to expect my call so when I introduced myself she knew who I was. We talked a lot by phone the first time, and then she invited me to her place. When I got there I was spell-bound. She was a beautiful woman. I found out she had been married and divorced. She had two young boys and was looking for a companion. She was a TV news anchor at the local television station. I was very attracted to her.

Over the next few weeks I spent a lot of time with Sarah. I wanted to be with her all the time. We went on dates, traveled to various sites and one Saturday, drove to the Oklahoma panhandle to take in an all-day Indian Pow-Wow. It was exciting to see the various tribes in their headdresses and native costumes. During all this time together, she indicated that she wanted sex, but being a strong Catholic at the time, I did not want to have sex out of marriage. I kept asking her to marry me, but she would object, saying it would be unfair to me with her two kids. I would counter-argue, and so it went.

One Sunday she invited me to go to church with her and the boys. She was a Sunday school teacher and asked if I would like to come along and observe. I met her at her house and we started kissing in her bedroom and I began to lose my restraint. She put me off saying we could do that after we got back from church. I attended the Sunday school with her and her boys. She introduced me to the class as a friend. The class went well and I was impressed with her even more than before. When we got back to her house, I had lost all desire for sex. We kept our relationship going for some time, but, eventually, we both realized it was not meant to be, so we broke up.

One of the guys from work played the violin. He heard that I played music, and asked if he could stop by some Friday night and bring his violin. I told him to come on over. He had only played classical music, but could read music very well. I had a lot of popular music books so I would play a song I knew and he would follow the music. It took a few minutes to work things out, but by the end of the evening, we were playing up a storm. He had never had so much fun. We did this several weeks and then it was time to go back to Colorado, since our training had come to an end.

Back in Denver, we kept in contact. He would come to my place and play, and I would take my accordion and go to his place and play. One Friday he begged me to come for dinner and we would play music as well. I had other plans, but he kept insisting, so I cancelled my previous plans and went to his home. When I got there, lo and behold was a Hammond Chord Organ. He had bought one just so I could play it whenever we got together. I couldn't believe it. After that, I spent most of my Friday nights at their place playing music.

My friend's wife was concerned that I didn't have a girlfriend. Her husband had a young, very attractive brunette working for him and suggested that I ask her for a date. He would have me come down to his area on a pretext of some sort so I could meet the young woman. Eventually, I asked her out.

I took her to a nice restaurant. We talked a lot. I began to like her and I assumed she liked me. The evening went great. I took her back to her apartment. We sat in the car for a couple minutes talking. I was about to ask her for another date when she said, "Well, I suppose you expect some sex. So come on up to my apartment."

I couldn't believe what I heard. It was like throwing ice water on me. I got angry and told her I did not expect that, and if that was how she felt, I wanted nothing to do with her. Another relationship ended even before it got started.

SITE TECHNICAL REPRESENTATIVE

When I got back to Martin-Marietta from Texas, there was no more need for instructors or training development, since the Air Force was now doing that. We were offered transfers to other divisions in the company where our talents or knowledge could be used. The best-paying position was that of a Technical Representative at one of the missile complexes near Denver. It utilized the knowledge and skills we already had, and would be a promotion. I became a Technical Representative (Tech Rep).

As a Tech Rep to the Air Force, I would be a resident expert they could call on if a problem occurred with the missile systems that they could not solve. It was essentially a boring job. I had an underground office at the missile site, and had no official duties until called upon to help solve a problem with the missile systems. I spent a lot of time brushing up on various missile operations, at first. Then spent time reading through various technical manuals, but after a while I began to get bored.

One of the biggest gripes I had about working at the silos was that the area was controlled by labor unions. To get something moved, we had to get a union person to do it. If we violated their rules, the union would complain and we would get in trouble. I hated it. It seemed so ridiculous to me. One time I wanted to move my wastebasket to the other side of my desk and had to wait until the request went up my chain of command to the union's chain of command to the actual person who came and moved the wastebasket. I complained to my management, but it did no good. The union was there and we could do nothing about it.

I got a call one night from my brother Buck. He was starting up a TV repair business and wanted to know if I'd be interested in going in business with him. He had a shop set up in the basement of his house. He would continue working his day job, but would do repair during the evenings and weekends and I could do it all the time. I said we could expand into CB Radios as well; something new and just beginning to take hold. As a result of our conversation, I quit my job and headed to Massachusetts. This was September 1961.

Radio and TV Repair (1961-1963)

Although Buck and I had grown up not very close, the last few years we had become so. Whenever I went back to New England to see friends and family, I always made it a point to spend time with Buck and his wife, Barb. Buck and I would reminisce about growing up in Maine, and some of our experiences. We enjoyed each other and I always looked forward to seeing him again.

At the right time of year, he and Barb would go catfishing. They caught Bullheads at night with a fishing pole and a lantern. I had never heard of that, so they invited me along one time. We sat on a river bank with fishing poles having baited lines in the water and a lantern to see our bait. It was quiet and a bit spooky, but we caught a lot of Bullheads that night. Buck showed me how to grab the Bullheads so I wouldn't get a barb in my hand or finger. I did okay for a first-timer. I offered to help clean them when we got back to Buck's place, but it was late and they said for me to go home and that they would clean them. They wanted me over the next night to see what the fish tasted like.

Next evening I was over to Buck and Barb's who had prepared a batch of catfish. I was reluctant to try any at first, never having tasted them before. As soon as I bit into the first one, I was convinced. I stuffed myself; Buck and Barb laughed.

That evening Buck showed me his workshop. He was well equipped to do radio and TV repair and had been working on equipment from friends and neighbors to get some experience, charging only the cost of parts. He had acquired sets of schematics to all the popular brands of TVs and radios, and had a good set of tools and test equipment. We needed to get paying customers, so Buck would canvas the area trying to drum up business while I repaired what we had in the shop. We tried to get contracts with TV and radio manufacturers to repair their equipment, but they already had contracts with shops.

Radios and TVs at this time had vacuum tubes and most people in the business didn't know how they worked. Our biggest competitor was a guy who owned a store selling RCA TVs, one of the most popular brands at the time. Since the majority of failures were caused by vacuum tubes, his method of repair was to replace one tube after another until he found the problem, charging the customer for all the tubes he replaced, even though only one was the problem. We called these people "Tube Jockeys." It was hard to compete with them because they never analyzed the problem, like we did. We charged only for the faulty part and our time, making us cheaper; however, they were usually faster, which made the customer happier (though poorer).

We could become "Tube Jockeys" ourselves, but we both felt it was dishonest. We needed a better way of building the business. I suggested to Buck that we go into CB radio sales and service. Citizen Band (CB) radio was just coming out and no one had that market yet. To repair any transmitter, you had to have a First Class Radio & Telephone license from the FCC. I had a self-teach course that prepared a person for the license, which I had been studying for some time. Buck liked the idea, so I gave him the course to study and in three months we went to Boston for the examination. I passed the test, but Buck did not. I told him it was okay, there would be another test in 3 months.

Since we only needed one person with a license, we decided to concentrate on getting the CB business going. The biggest buyers of CBs were truckers and small businesses. We contacted three CB manufacturers to see if we could be their local representative by selling and repairing their products locally. We wanted exclusive rights within an area of 20 miles surrounding Townsend, Massachusetts. All three manufacturers liked the idea but we had to always have a minimum inventory of CB models and replacement parts. They would provide advertising posters, pamphlets and news announcements for our store and would pay all the radio and TV advertising in the area for the first three months; after that we would share the cost.

Buck and I were ecstatic. This could be really big; however, we didn't have the money to even buy sample CBs. Buck was willing to get a loan from the bank, but Barb was not. I thought if we could buy a few units to demonstrate, then maybe we could begin making sales; I put together a Marketing Plan to take to a bank to see if we could get a loan that way.

I met with a young Vice President at the bank and explained that we would be leasing CB units to customers which included maintenance. Our plan was to simply replace a bad unit so the customer could go on his way with minimum delay. We would then repair the bad unit at our leisure and place it back in inventory as a future replacement unit. No one was doing that kind of service and we were sure we would beat any competition.

The young VP liked the idea a lot. We were asking for $25,000. He said he was not authorized to make that big of a loan. He would talk to his senior VP and for me to come back the next day. The Senior VP liked the idea also, but he wasn't about to give us money without us investing some of our own. He said to buy some units and try the idea for three to six months and if we were selling products and acquiring customers, he'd be glad to give us a loan.

Dad heard about our plight and said he had $1500.00 he would give me to get started. I told him I might not be able to pay him back. He said that if the business goes, to pay him back then. I took the money and bought a base CB unit, transmitter, antenna and three portable CB units. We found we could talk about 5 miles away from each other with the units.

Before we started our ad campaign and sales effort, Buck, Dennis and I decided to give the portable CB units a good test. We were going bird hunting and took the units along to test them out. We found that the units worked very well, even when we were some distance from each other. At the end of the day's hunt, we met back at our vehicles and bragged about how good the units were. From there, we were all going to meet back at Buck's. Buck and I took off but there was no Dennis for quite a while. When he showed up he said he had put his CB unit on top of his car while he was putting away his hunting rifle. Then he got into the car and drove off, forgetting the CB unit was on top. He heard it slide off the roof and stopped the car. The unit had hit the ground and shattered.

That same evening Barb announced that she would be running the business, taking care of the office, taking orders and the various paperwork so that Buck and I would be free from these tasks. Apparently, she had convinced Buck because my complaints went unheeded. I let it be known if that was the way it was going to be, I no longer wanted to be part of the business. *As I look back, I see God's hand in this.*

Philco Technical Representative (1963)

I had been staying with Mom and Dad (and Vincent) and had not been able to help with household expenses. I got a job at a radio station in Manchester, New Hampshire, as a technician, but spent my time being a disc jockey. I began paying Mom and Dad some money every week to help offset household expenses.

I wanted to get back into industrial electronics. I really wanted to save up some money to come back and get the CB business going. The quickest way of doing that was to get a job with RCA working on the Distant Early Warning (DEW) line in northern Alaska. There I could sock away my pay because my food and shelter were provided at no cost. I figured I could save up $25,000 in a couple years.

RCA responded with a letter that in effect said they were now only hiring Alaskan natives for the DEW line. The only other response I got was from the Philco Corporation. Their Technical Representative division was in need of Basic Electronics instructors to teach at the Great Lakes Naval Training Station in North Chicago, Illinois. I got the job. This was April 1963.

Philco required all new-hires to report to their Philadelphia headquarters for three days of orientation before going to their assignment. Because they had many transients throughout the year, Philco contracted with places that provided food and lodging for a few days at a time. The place I was lodging at was in the home of a little old lady who cooked and cleaned. After I returned from a day's orientation, she would prepare dinner and we would talk while we ate. The last evening I was there she announced to me that I would be married before the end of the year. I laughed and said that was impossible, that I didn't even know a girl I would marry. She said not to laugh, that it would happen.

North Chicago, where the Naval Training Station is located, is next to Waukegan. I found lodging at the Waukegan YMCA. I began teaching at the Naval Training Station and became friends with a few of the instructors. One friend in particular had been with Philco for a number of years. He spent his weekends going to a bar, buying one drink and observing people. I spent one time doing that with him but wasn't too interested in continuing. We would do other things together, like take in a movie or just sit and talk. As it turned out, most of my weekends were spent with him.

PAMELA

Since my friend at work had been with Philco a long time, he had vacation coming. He would be gone over the 4th of July weekend, so I looked in the paper to see how I might spend my time. I liked to bowl and had been in leagues all the way back to the time in the Air Force. The local paper said that there was going to be a Dutch Doubles at a local bowling alley that Saturday. I called the bowling alley to see if I needed a partner to participate. They said I did not; that they would pair me up with someone.

I got to the bowling alley and was paired with someone else. Dutch Doubles is where you and your partner alternate balls all the way through the game. It's a fun way of meeting people and not getting too serious about your score. Each doubles pair bowled another doubles pair.

As it turned out, on the doubles pair we bowled against was Pam. I thought she was the most beautiful girl I had ever seen. We talked a bit but I was too bashful to get her full name and telephone number. That evening I wanted to kick myself for not getting her telephone number. That Sunday I drove up and down the streets of Waukegan hoping to see her going to church.

For the next few weeks, I continued to teach and we formed a bowling team at work and bowled each Wednesday evening at the other bowling alley in Waukegan. We didn't use up all the alleys with our league, so there was always a few unused lanes that were open to the public. One Wednesday evening as I was bowling, I looked over and there was Pam bowling by herself. I immediately jumped over the ball return and asked if she remembered me. She said she did. I asked her to slow down, that I wanted to bowl with her. When I walked back to my league there were all my friends staring at me and began to tease, which, in this case, I enjoyed.

After bowling with Pam that night, I made sure to get her telephone number and address. I was elated how things worked out. We both had our own bowling balls and bag. I picked up the two bags and went to the parking lot. We came to my car first, so I set my bag down behind my car and walked to her car. I placed the bag in her car and set up a date to pick her up a few days later. She drove away. I was so excited I ran to my car, started it up and proceeded to back over my bowling bag!

Pam and I began dating a lot. For me, it was love at first sight. I found out later that it was the same for her. I would pick up Pam at her house. She would come out, so I never met her mother or any relatives at that point in time. We talked a lot and would go to a restaurant or a movie. She was only twenty years old. Her Dad had died when she was sixteen. She was much closer to her Dad than to her mother (Hazel). Her Dad had been a Civil Engineer for Waukegan, so he was well known and respected. Hazel had always planned for Pam to marry into a rich family. As our dating continued, Pam and Hazel were having more and more arguments about me.

When her mother saw that Pam and I were getting serious about each other, she invited me over for a Sunday dinner, to get acquainted. The dinner went well with questions about my work and my family. After dinner, as I was helping bring dishes into the kitchen, Hazel cornered me and wanted to know my finances and what my means of support were for her daughter, should we get married. I looked her right in the face and told her that the means of support was me. She didn't like that, but I didn't care. I thanked them for dinner, set up a date with Pam and left the house.

During the next few weeks, I was investigated by Hazel's sister and brother-in-law, who worked for the Waukegan Sheriff's department. Since I held a Secret Clearance in the military and also with Martin-Marietta, I had already been highly investigated and had a clean slate; not even a traffic ticket. This frustrated Hazel and her sister, so they began scheming on how to get me or Pam to change our minds.

A week later, I was invited over to Pam's house to meet some of the relatives. There were aunts and uncles and cousins, all curious to know more about me. After an hour or so of questions, the relatives left except for a favorite cousin of Pam's, who I will call Zee and his wife Dee. Dee and Hazel disappeared to the kitchen while Zee began talking to Pam and me. He did everything he could to try and discourage our continued relationship. I was eight years older than Pam. I was a Catholic, she was a Lutheran. I had only begun working for Philco a few months; and so it went on and on. He thought because he and Pam were close that he could talk her out of it. He succeeded in ending their close relationship and strengthening Pam's and mine.

At work, we were told that Philco had lost the contract with the Navy. Since I was a new hire, I would be let go. My work would end the last week of October. That same weekend, Control Data came to Waukegan looking for technical instructors for their expanding computer business in Minnesota. I interviewed and was hired on the spot, with a start date of December 3, 1963. *Coincidence? I don't think so.*

I was now more determined than ever to marry Pam. I felt that if we were not married before I moved to Minnesota, we probably wouldn't get married. I bought an engagement/wedding ring combination. I asked her out to dinner at the best restaurant in Waukegan, one that her parents had frequented for years, so Pam was well known there. I left the ring in the glove compartment of my car. We had dinner and I was nervous. I realized that leaving the ring in the car was stupid. I didn't know how I was going to go get the ring and propose. Like a fool I pretended to have an argument with her and walked out of the restaurant, leaving her dumbfounded and with the bill.

I quickly got the ring and returned to the restaurant and walked to the booth where she was still sitting, not knowing what to do. I placed the ring on the table in front of her, held her hand and asked her to marry me. The biggest smile came across her face as she blurted out: "Yes! Yes!" I apologized for being so stupid. She brushed it off as she was putting on the ring. She proudly went to the owners, showed them the ring and announced she was getting married. They came over to the booth to meet me and took the bill, saying their congratulations and that the meal was on the house.

I wanted to be married in the Catholic Church in Waukegan. I found out that to marry Pam in the church, she would have to take seven Catechism lessons. I told her about it and she agreed.

I went to the church to set up the lessons and to pin down a date for the wedding. The head priest said he would not marry us even though she would be taking the lessons. Another priest, Father Carolan, overheard the conversation, took me aside and asked me about Pam. He then agreed to give the lessons and to marry us. We set the wedding date for November 16, about two months away.

At Pam's second of seven Catechism lessons, she let Father Carolan know that her mother wanted nothing to do with the wedding. She was against it. Father Carolan said for Pam to invite him over the next Sunday afternoon, and for as many relatives as could to be there; he wanted to meet them and talk to them. That Sunday afternoon, Pam's house was full of relatives. Father Carolan met everyone then proceeded to explain why this was a good marriage. The fact that I had an established career and that I was 28 years of age were all positive. I was past the age of trying to find out who I was and what I wanted. There were no objections voiced. Before Father Carolan left, Hazel had agreed to take care of the invitations and the wedding breakfast. The battle was finally over.

We were married on Saturday, November 16, 1963. There was a good attendance from Pam's relatives and friends. No one from my side of the family came. Before the ceremony started, I was so nervous. My best man and I were in a small room near the altar. He did the best he could to calm me down. When the music started, my friend and I went in front of the railing before the altar and waited for Pam and her escorts to get there. The ceremony went well. I often remember the old lady in Philadelphia who said I would be married before the end of the year. *Again, God's hand in my life.*

When Pam and I got to my car, we found it marked with a "Just Married" sign and a string of cans tied by rope to the back bumper. We made our way to the wedding breakfast, meeting and greeting a lot of people. Hazel's sister, Helen, and her husband didn't come to the wedding or the breakfast, showing their continued disapproval of me. As soon as we could, Pam and I left the wedding breakfast and started our honeymoon to Townsend, Massachusetts, to visit my parents.

Move to Minnesota (1963)

During the honeymoon trip to Townsend, Massachusetts, we were visited by my brothers, Buck and Dennis, and their families. Vincent was still going to school and still living with Mom and Dad. Pam and I took a quick trip to Mars Hill so she could meet my brother Dick, his wife Lorraine and their families.

On the day we said goodbye to Mom and Dad to leave, Dad handed me a 100 dollar bill as a wedding present. It would prove to be a Godsend; we were heading for Minnesota, a new life and a new job.

As we were crossing Ohio, I noticed something odd. The sun was shining, so I put on my sunglasses as I drove the car. A few minutes later, it became overcast and began to sprinkle, so I removed the sunglasses. A few minutes after that, the sun came out again. This repeated itself several times. I began to laugh. Pam asked what I was laughing at, so I told her what had been happening with the sunglasses and weather. She said I was just imagining things. So I told her to watch what happens. Over the next half hour or so, I would put on my sunglasses and it would start to rain; I would take the glasses off and the sun would come out. She asked how come that was happening. I told her I didn't know, but God must have a sense of humor. I took off the glasses and traveled in sunlight the rest of that day. This incident with the sun and the rain would happen many times in my life after that. I always felt that God needed a good laugh once in a while and I was eager to please Him.

When we got to Minnesota, we found a motel with a kitchen, where we planned to stay until we could find an apartment. It was Sunday, the day before I reported to work. Pam and I went shopping for kitchen utensils. Most all the stores were closed on Sunday. We were a bit desperate and kept driving around until we found a drug store that was open until noon. They had the things we needed, but that area of the store was cordoned off. We asked what was going on. They said that on Sunday, only the pharmacy area was open. The law prevented them from selling other items on Sundays. We explained our plight and the owner let us get some cooking supplies and utensils. Incidentally, a few years later Target Stores challenged the law in court and won, causing most of the Sunday restrictions to be removed.

Pam and I realized that we were nearly out of money and I wouldn't get my first paycheck for two weeks. There was a convenience store nearby so I told her to go there when I was gone on Monday and pick up whatever she could get to hold us over until payday. When I came home I found that she had bought a box of cereal, a loaf of bread, a gallon of milk, a dozen eggs, a small jar of jam, a package of baloney and a small bottle of mustard. She had a little money left and insisted that I take it for work. I used it to buy a cup of coffee each day to go with my baloney sandwich.

Control Data (1963–1987)

My 24-year career at Control Data, allowed me to grow in responsibilities while providing me with a wide range of experiences. I was hired as a technical instructor and would be teaching at a facility in downtown Minneapolis. Control Data headquarters were in Bloomington, a suburb of Minneapolis, where I was reporting during my orientation. After three days, I began traveling to Minneapolis. There would be more than 50 newly-hired instructor employees during the next few months. Some were assigned to teach basic electronics and others, including myself, to teach existing computer maintenance courses. When I saw that they were teaching from wiring diagrams, I felt I had stepped back in time. I told my boss about logic diagrams that were used on the Titan missile program. He liked the idea and assigned me to develop such diagrams for an existing training course. To do that, I would have to meet with the design engineers of that computer.

I was paid twice a month. With my first paycheck we were able to set aside money needed for an apartment. Pam and I found one near a convenience store half a block away and the rent was what we could afford, so we took the apartment and moved.

One day I had to report to headquarters for a briefing. Pam had gone to the convenience store to get some groceries. After the briefing I was to report back to the training facility in Minneapolis. Since it was lunchtime and my trip took me past the apartment, I decided to surprise Pam and have lunch with her at the apartment. There was snow on the ground, but it was melting, making the snow slushy. The street I took dead-ended on the street our apartment was on, but near the convenience store. As I was approaching the street, I could see Pam carrying two full paper bags of groceries. Ahead of me was a guy in a Volkswagen. Just as he got to the street ahead of me, one of the paper bags Pam was carrying let go and groceries went everywhere. The guy in the Volkswagen stopped to help her, but she didn't know what to do. I drove up, tooted my horn and the biggest relief came over her face when she saw me. I believe the Lord put it in my mind to have lunch with Pam, just for this reason.

I worked as a Course Developer/Instructor for several years. The company's computer products were popular with universities and large businesses. We were competitive with IBM, computer sales were increasing, and, as a result, the company was rapidly growing.

We lived in a one bedroom apartment in Richfield near the Airport. It took a while, but we eventually ignored the airplanes taking off and landing.

Pam was pregnant with Joan. I remember Pam telling me it was time to go. She was very calm, I was very nervous. We made it to the hospital where I waited, and waited. After 25 hours in labor, the doctors discovered that Pam's bones were too narrow for the baby to be born normally; they needed to do a Caesarian Section (C-section). I got some more coffee and continued to pace. Joan was born on September 5, 1964 at 2:20 in the afternoon.

FIRST HOUSE

Pam and I bought our first house in Apple Valley. It was a three bedroom with unfinished basement.

Before we moved into the house, I remember working on the house for hours to get it ready for moving in. It was about eight p.m. when I was washing the bathroom window. I had raised the lower window and was sitting with my legs hanging out. I was so happy that we had a house that I didn't realize how long I was gone. I could see the front street through the window I was washing when I noticed a police car stop in front of the house. The cop got out of the car, walked to below me and asked if I was Carlton. I said that I was. He said that my wife was worried about me since I had been gone so long (no cell phones back then). He had her on his two-way radio and asked me to come and speak with her, which I did.

Pam became pregnant again. I was hoping for a boy. I couldn't be with Pam at the hospital because I was taking care of Joan. Pam said as soon the baby was born she would have a nurse call me at home. Finally a call came informing me it was a boy (Michael) born at 10:02 a.m. November 1, 1965. I was ecstatic. I hung up the phone and proceeded to jump over a fence I had across the top of the stairs, luckily landing on my feet and hitting the entrance wall with my back. Good thing the house was a split level.

Pam and I had been going to a Catholic Church in the Apple Valley area. With two young children, and my time at work (I would often work part of Saturdays), we went as often as we could. At this time we were unable to save any money. It seemed any time we got a little ahead, an extra expense came along and gobbled it up.

I want to insert here why I was working so much. I did not have a college degree and I was competing against people with degrees. I felt it necessary to do the best I could in every job, including working extra hours, to compete. I was usually the first at work and often the last to leave. This made me stand out as an employee, but it had its toll on my family, especially Pam.

The Catholic Church was having a building drive. They wanted to expand the Rectory. According to the priest, whenever a visiting priest or bishop came, the priest had to sleep in the attic (that sounds familiar, except Dennis and I did it all the time years before). The Sunday that the drive started, everyone was given a sales kit. This consisted of magazine advertisements, envelopes for money, a roster for recording magazine customers, and a schedule for making sales.

After we got home, Pam and I went through the sales kit and both realized we didn't have the time to do any selling. Part of our problem was that several of our neighbors were Catholics, making our sales area more limited. The following Monday evening, I called the priest and mentioned that we would not be able to do any selling. His first response was that because of us he would have to continue staying in the attic whenever company came.

This made me angry. I told him that with my work schedule and Pam at home with two young kids; we didn't have the time to do any selling. His response this time was that we would have to put in the money equivalent to all twenty subscriptions. I told him if that was his attitude, we would no longer be coming to his church. That was the end of my being a Catholic. I started doing Bible Study more intently. I bought a King James Version of the Bible to compare verses that I studied. With our lives busy as it was, my Bible Study time was limited. Worldly tasks were crowding out my relationship with God.

At this time there was much interest in smaller computers that would provide monitoring and control of various factory functions. Soon Control Data came out with such a smaller computer, which was desk sized instead of room sized. This new computer, the 3400, was far cheaper than a typical mainframe. Because of that, many computers could be purchased more cheaply to handle a manufacturing process than a multimillion dollar mainframe. Many 3400s could be set up along a large process, thereby reducing production time and cost while maintaining high quality.

The high demand for the 3400 presented a training problem; there was no computer set aside for training. Unless a customer service technician visited the manufacturing plant, the technician would go into the field without ever having seen a 3400.

I developed the maintenance course for the 3400 and began teaching this course. It was the first course to completely eliminate wiring diagrams. We had improved logic diagrams to the extent that everything needed to maintain a computer was included in the logic diagram.

Early on there was a technician who had been trained on the 3400, but had never seen one. He knew it was desk sized. He was called into a customer's facility to repair a recently-purchased 3400. The owner met him at the door, pointed toward a door down the hallway, and told him he had to make a phone call. He said he would join the technician as soon as he could.

About ten minutes later, the owner comes into the room to find the technician taking apart the air conditioner. The owner told the technician to get off the property. He immediately called the Control Data CEO, who sent out another technician, but also authorized that the Training Department should get one each of the computers being trained on. I had learned a long time before that an instructor cannot rightfully claim a student can perform a task unless he sees it being demonstrated by the student. Having a computer on which to demonstrate legitimized our training.

Control Data was selling hundreds of the 3400 computers. I had a second instructor trained to help with the teaching load. About a year after I started teaching the 3400 course, Control Data sold 50 of them to Motorola for their plant in Phoenix, Arizona. Because I had developed the course, the sales representative who made the sale wanted me and my family to come out to Phoenix for a month so I could teach the course to Motorola personnel, who would be maintaining the computers.

Pam and I drove to Phoenix in February, taking a southern route. It was quite a change for us, leaving snow and cold for 80-degree weather. Joan was over two years old and Mike was a few months old. We met the sales rep who told us where we would be staying for the month. When we got there, they had no vacancies. We called the sales rep, who told us to go to a motel for the night and he would have a place for us by the next day. True to his word, he found a 3-story, furnished 3-bedroom apartment. That was part of a complex with a pool. It was far more than we needed, but under the circumstances, and the fact that it was all being paid by Control Data, we were not going to complain. After settling in, we went down to the pool. Even though Joan had never been in a pool, she was a natural swimmer. So Joan and I or Pam and Joan would take turns swimming together.

Pam was claustrophobic and wouldn't go into an elevator. When I was at work, she would fill a diaper bag, put it on the elevator and press the button for the first floor. Then she would go down the stairs, carrying Mike in her arms and holding onto Joan's hand. When she got to the first floor, she would retrieve the diaper bag from the elevator. On her way back up, she did the opposite.

Going down to the pool made a good break in the day for Pam. One day she worked up the nerve to go on the elevator. She noticed that there was a maintenance man on the elevator too. About halfway down, the elevator stopped unexpectedly. Pam was panicking. The maintenance man told her it was nothing; he would have it fixed in no time. After the elevator was fixed, Pam never went on any elevators the rest of her life; no matter the number of steps, she would walk.

Motorola wanted me to come and work for them, offering me a considerable salary increase. Pam and I talked about it, but it was such a change in climate that I didn't think I would ever enjoy it there. I turned down the offer and returned to Minnesota. In my spare time I began finishing off the basement. Pam's mother was retiring and wasn't sure where she was going to live. We invited her to live with us. She accepted and now I had to go into high gear to complete another bedroom in the basement.

I enjoyed working on the basement. It was a chance to add needed space and increase equity in the house. When I was done I had a Family Room, Bathroom, and two bedrooms in the basement. We had Michael move to a basement bedroom and Pam's mother (Hazel) moved into Michael's bedroom upstairs.

The house had a split entry and its location was within walking distance of the school the kids would go to. I eventually put in a big garden and enjoyed working it in my spare time.

Pam and I had not had much of a chance to go out, being busy with children and the house. After Hazel moved in, Pam and I began going out for an occasional dinner. Over time, it worked well that Hazel was with us. It was good for the kids and Hazel to know each other, and good for us as well.

Pam became pregnant again, which was a concern. Her doctor had said that each subsequent childbirth by C-section was more and more difficult on the body. She decided that after this birth there would be no more. On August 21, 1967, Sally was born at 9:22 p.m. At the recommendation of her doctor, Pam had a hysterectomy some months later.

During the mid and late sixties, there was a shortage of people with technical backgrounds who qualified for hiring candidates to maintain computers. Companies were stealing from other companies, but the pool of qualified candidates was limited and not growing as rapidly as the computer industry demanded. Control Data decided to create a technical school (Control Data Institute, CDI) primarily to teach basic electronics and computer fundamentals. Graduates from this school would begin satisfying the growing demand for qualified recruits into the computer industry. Although graduates were free to go to any computer company, the availability of qualified candidates helped Control Data as well.

I was transferred to CDI to begin development of a Basic Electronics training manual to be used by the institute. Besides the training manual, there was an Instructor's Guide and a host of multimedia that had to be developed to accompany the course. Up until that time, except for small pockets within the company, all typing and graphics production was farmed out to outside businesses. I made a proposal to the head of CDI that there be a graphics production organization in CDC to satisfy all the needs of Control Data. I told him it would save costs and keep all production under our control. He wanted me to prove the costs savings by doing the Basic Electronic Training Manual internally. He had an external quote to which he would compare the results.

I hired two typists and knew of a graphic artist in the company who was eager to do any graphics I needed. Input came from Instructor/Developers who were handwriting the manual's content. I took over the role of editor to coordinate all the activities and to finalize the manual. As a result, the manual was produced in three months (instead of six) at a savings of several thousand dollars. The head of CDI was impressed and approved my Graphics Development department, with me as the manager. I asked my graphic artist friend to join the department, which he did. In addition to the two existing typists, I hired two lesser experienced typists to convert the handwriting inputs to type, making it far more efficient for the higher-paid typists to produce final copy from already-typed manuscripts.

A little story about one of the lesser-experienced typists I hired. She had just graduated from high school and would also type up my memos and letters, to give her additional typing experience. She was slow and made a lot of mistakes. She was located just outside my office. One day she yelled for me to come and see what she was doing. I came out of my office and watched her typing faster than I had ever seen before. When she saw me she said, "Look, I can type without looking at the keyboard!" She eventually became one of my better production typists.

A little side note. Before printing the Basic Electronics manual, I had edited it several times and was content that it was error free. When the first manuals arrived from the printer, I grabbed a copy, brought it to the head of CDI and boldly defied him to find an error. He smiled, seemed impressed at the looks of the manual and then randomly opened the book. He scanned the page and immediately found a typo. I have never made such a claim since then. I guess I was getting cocky and needed to be taken down a peg or two.

I put the word out about my department's capabilities and solicited work from other places within the company. As time went on we grew to a staff of fifteen people, doing work for departments throughout the company. We became known for our quality, on-time delivery and cost savings.

Our marriage was doing well at this time. Although I was at work a lot, I spent time with the family when I was home. I would take Pam out to dinner or a show quite often. Having Pam's mother living with us provided Pam with help as she needed it. Our sexual relationship was the best it had ever been. Life was good.

During my time with the Graphics Production department, the head of CDI approached me one day and asked if I would meet with him about a special project he had in mind. At the meeting, he had a representative from a company that manufactured 16mm movie projectors. Unlike any other projectors at that time, this one could be programmed to not only show movies, but single frames, and could go forward or backward from any frame to any frame. With 4000 frames on a typical 16mm reel, this provided a lot of capacity for a variety of projections. By advancing one frame at a time, an instructor could use it in place of overhead transparencies. By being able to go from any frame to any frame, there could be a mix of still images with movies. Not only classroom instruction, but individualized instruction could be accommodated where the machine would bypass material the student already covered, or material could be repeated for reinforcement.

Things were going good in the Graphics Production department. I had a person trained to fill in for me whenever I was gone. This project sounded like a lot of fun and I was interested in individualized instruction, so I took on the assignment.

The movie projector company had been working with a design engineer in CDC who had been studying the machine for a while, so I went over to meet him. He had produced a few images on film to check out the programming. He showed me how it could go one frame at a time, forward or backward. He hadn't developed a movie to insert, and was doing most of his work on his own time. He showed me the tool for programming the film. It was a copy camera, with the center for the picture, or graphic, and the edge of the film for coding instructions and imprinting frame numbers. There was a code for moving forward any number of frames and a different code for moving backward any number of frames. There was a code for projecting one frame at a time and a different code for projecting a movie. Through the use of these and other codes, an instructor could have the projector do whatever was needed.

I told him I was going to develop a short training session using still images and a movie that would exploit all the features of the projector. He said he was interested, and to keep him in the loop. One day he told me that the reason he was interested was that he wanted to eventually develop a device where the user would be immersed into the program. He saw individualized instruction as a way of getting there. I often wondered, later, if he was involved in the development of virtual reality devices we have today.

The subject had to be reasonably short and of interest. CDC wanted to demonstrate what I came up with at a trade show in San Francisco, a few months away. I called a Biology professor at the University of Minnesota, told him what I needed and asked if there was anything he knew about that might be appropriate for my needs. He said, "How about Reptiles of Minnesota". There were not that many, so it wouldn't exceed the capacity of the 16mm reel. There could be stills. I said I needed a short movie. He suggested showing a snake eating a mouse. He said his snake only ate about once a month, but should be doing so again in a few days. We set up a day to do filming at the university in hopes of getting the snake and mouse movie.

Meanwhile I hired a consultant to do the programming of the film. The projector company provided a projector and copy camera and instructions to the consultant. I had him meet with the design engineer, to pick his brains and bring the design engineer up to speed on our project. We went to the university to meet with the biologist and pick up photographs of various Minnesota reptiles, so he could get started on an introduction to the subject matter.

A few days later the biologist called and said that they would be feeding the snake and I should be able to get a movie of it. I hired a camera crew and went to the university. The biologist hoped that the snake would eat, but he couldn't promise it. The camera crew set up flood lights and two cameras. Then checked their equipment and gave the okay to proceed. The mouse was placed in the snake's cage, but nothing happened. Five minutes went by, still nothing. I was getting concerned, since I was paying the camera crew by the hour. I expressed my concern to the Biologist; he asked to give it a little more time. He thought the spot lights would warm up the snake and increase his appetite. A few minutes later, the snake attacked the mouse and slowly swallowed it. We had our movie.

We got our project done, made a few copies of the 16mm reel and sent everything out with the sales representatives to San Francisco, where it was one of the hits at the trade show. It was a nice side project for me. I went back to the Graphics Department.

I found out later that the 16mm projector project was scrapped as being too mechanical and impractical. CDC was working with the 3M Company, who, in turn, was working with Philips to develop a device that would put sound and video onto a disc, but that was a few years away before it would have commercial value.

The institute decided to use videotapes for motion pictures. At the time, VHS and Betamax were competing formats.[4] We selected the Betamax format because of its compactness and better quality. Later we would convert to videodiscs.

I made a proposal to the CDI director that we consider exploring individualized instruction as a cost-effective way of training. He thought that might be a good idea, so he sent me to the University of Michigan where they were holding a week long seminar on individualized instruction.

After hearing what was being done in other places with individualized instruction, I came back pumped up to get something started. I couldn't get anyone interested. I became frustrated and began looking around for a new job. A new department was being formed to provide multimedia courses to colleges and universities. They needed someone who could create and manage a distribution department and write procedures related to all their activities. I took on the job.

During this time, I had joined Bible Study Fellowship (BSF), a men's group meeting every Monday evening during fall, winter and spring. It was a large group of about 150 people. The large group would be divided into smaller groups of up to 20 people each with a Bible Study leader for each group. My leader was Doug Hansen. He and I soon became close friends and would have prayer breakfasts together Monday mornings, if time permitted.

I got a small crew together to handle the storage and distribution of multimedia products for colleges and universities. I rented a 4000 square foot warehouse to hold the products, wrote procedures for the various duties as well as procedures to assure orders were legitimate.

Once a week I would attend a meeting of the organization, where each department head gave a report of status and problems.

At one meeting, our boss said that he wanted all the departments to put together their proposals for how the organization should be restructured and what the future product set would be. I was given the task of documenting our future product set. The boss wanted our documents and presentations to be provided at the following Wednesday 10 O'clock staff meeting. He would provide the minutes from today's meeting later that day, which would include each person's assignment. One of the people within the department came to me after the meeting and told me she had been interfacing with the outside organization that was supposed to provide us with new products, but none were forthcoming. Now I was in a quandary. This was Monday, with less than two days to go and nothing to document.

That evening at BSF we studied in Kings how, when Hezekiah was king, the city of Jerusalem was surrounded by the Assyrian army. They sent a letter to Hezekiah to surrender. He took the letter to the synagogue, placed the letter down in front of him and prayed to God concerning his predicament.

2Ki 19:14 *And Hezekiah received the letter of the hand of the messengers, and read it: and Hezekiah went up into the house of the LORD, and spread it before the LORD.* That night God sent His angels throughout the Assyrian camp, killing 185,000 of them.

The following morning when I got to work, I took the memo of the meeting, placed it on my desk and prayed to God about it. I asked for direction and whatever help I would need to get my part of the task done. I would leave it in His capable hands.

That day everyone in the department except me was scrambling to get their presentations documented. I proceeded to go about my normal duties. By the end of the day, nothing had come concerning new products. I went home, confident in the Lord, but a bit concerned. The presentation would be tomorrow at 10 a.m. and I had nothing to present. That night I prayed to the Lord again, expressing my concern, but leaving the matter with Him.

Wednesday morning, people in the department came early to work to complete their presentations. It was like a beehive with people running back and forth. I continued working on my usual tasks, getting a bit more concerned.

At nine O'clock, a special meeting was called for the entire department to inform us that our organization was being disbanded, with parts being incorporated within other departments. Most of the personnel (including me) would be transferring to other parts of CDC. *It was here that I learned to wait on the Lord.* Someone at BSF once said that God may not be early, but He is never late.

I was transferred, along with my distribution staff, to a new organization that would be acquiring and selling training products and services to higher education institutions. A business plan had been put together that identified the needs of these institutions, and we were to provide products and services that would meet those needs.

Control Data had developed the PLATO System as a way of using computers to teach lessons. Lessons were stored on a supercomputer and accessed from remote terminals. Several universities had acquired the computers and had networked their computers together, making it easier for research. This crude network would eventually lead to what we enjoy today as the Internet.

CDC was heavily promoting PLATO and provided a terminal for employee's homes so they could become familiar with it. I had a terminal in my home and had the kids use it. There were basic instructional packages and some games that they enjoyed playing. Sally was about nine years old and one of her favorite instructional programs was a math game with a bumble bee in it.

I had mentioned this to one of my workmates, who was a PLATO sales representative. She was intrigued that a nine year old could use the system. PLATO was going to be demonstrated at a trade show in Washington DC. I was also going to be on vacation with the family in New England at that time. She asked if it would be possible to stop by the trade show for a day or two and have Sally demo the PLATO System.

As long as it did not reduce our vacation time and the costs while in Washington DC were picked up by the company, I told her I'd be glad to do it. Since I was familiar with PLATO, my role would be to help the sales reps during the time that Sally was there. This all worked out to everyone's benefit.

We drove to Washington DC, staying at the hotel where the trade show was being held. During our free time we had a chance to ride around DC and see some of the sites.

At the trade show, they had Sally sit on a high stool in the front of the booth, visible to all who walked by. She just simply played her favorite "Bee" math game. The sales rep was touting the fact that PLATO was so easy to use that a child could operate it, pointing to Sally. It made an impression, with many talking with Sally as well. This was all before the advent of the personal computer.

After our two days in Washington DC, we headed for New England and started our vacation.

At one meeting, we found out that the City University of New York (CUNY) wanted learning carrels to house the multimedia equipment needed for the courses. A friend of mine and I jumped at the chance to take on the project.

We went to CUNY to find out how they were to use the carrels and the size needed, along with other information. We got a proposal from them for a learning center housing 50 carrels to be placed near a large library where the multimedia products would be stored and checked out.

With that information, we designed carrels with audiotape, videotape, and slide projector equipment housed in a compartment behind a small video monitor and projector screen built into the wall behind the student's writing desk. Sound from the audiotape and videotape devices was connected into headsets within the carrel. Carrel size accommodated two people, the student and, when needed, an instructor or assistant. The equipment compartment had a fan to keep the equipment from overheating. Once we had the design completed, we had a local carpenter build a prototype. We took the disassembled prototype to CUNY, assembled it and demonstrated its functionality. We completed the project and ended up selling 50 of the carrels to CUNY.

One day, our boss called me and my friend who helped design the learning carrels, into his office. He said he had just been contacted by the St. Cloud State University (SCSU) to send representatives to the university who could be involved in preparing a document which would try and predict how education would be provided in the year 2000 (this was the year 1975). We would be meeting once a month over the next year to document our ideas concerning learning technology at that future date. We told our boss that we wanted to be part of this planning group. He approved our involvement as officially representing

Control Data. We had to do most of our work in our spare time, but CDC would pay any direct expenses.

My friend and I would meet in our spare time and do a lot of brainstorming. We figured that there would be video discs and much more individualized instruction. We documented our thoughts on how instructions could be provided in learning carrels, much like CUNY was doing.

The head of the project was Doug Johnson from St. Cloud State University (SCSU). He headed up a special needs training function at the university and was excited to have our involvement. He wanted to use whatever we came up with as a planning document for the university, so that they would be in a better position to provide such futuristic training. It was a fun project and Doug was an energetic and committed individual. He could pull whatever resources from the university that might be needed for our project.

Doug and I became good friends and whenever he was in town Pam and I would have him over for dinner. Doug should have been a dean at the university by then; however, he had not completed his PhD. All he needed to do was complete his oral final exam, but never was motivated to do it. It seemed that he preferred his present position at the university than to be promoted out of it.

We completed the project in the form of a written document which incorporated our ideas and those from people at the university. The university provided information on how people learned and many of the techniques that Doug was using in his special needs training. My friend and I provided our ideas on what technology would be available and the manner of implementing individualized instruction. Copies were given to my friend and I as well as some to be distributed to higher management within CDC. (Incidentally, Doug died a few years after the project ended. I remember him as someone wholly committed to education, and a dear friend.)

In addition to my normal duties, I was also writing procedures for people in all areas of the organization. I liked it, because it enabled me to understand the whole organization. At one of the weekly meetings, someone asked a "What if question." The Vice President (VP) said "Don't worry about it, its Carney's job to clean the crap that falls to the bottom of the birdcage." Several people snickered but I kept my cool and didn't react. After the meeting was over I confronted the VP about his comment. He said it had to do with my procedure writing; that I would resolve the problem in the procedure. I told him he could have chosen far better words to get the point across. I told him I would begin looking for work elsewhere in the company. It was the end of the day. I went home both hurt and angry.

That night I prayed to the Lord and a verse in Romans came to mind: *Rom 12:19 Dearly beloved, avenge not yourselves, but rather give place unto wrath: for it is written, Vengeance is mine; I will repay, saith the Lord.* I prayed for the Lord to take whatever vengeance concerning the VP He felt appropriate. I would leave it in His hands.

The VP of the organization and his sales General Manager were under pressure to meet certain sales goals by the end of the year. By some miracle, they made their goals and received considerable bonuses for their achievement. They even held an expensive, catered Christmas party for all the employees involved and their spouses. Pam and I went. She was not at all impressed by either the sales General Manager or the Vice President. She felt that they were both self-centered, conveying a superior attitude, especially the VP. He liked smoking cigars and didn't care if it offended anyone. He tried to convince Pam to talk me into staying with the group. She told him that I made decisions about my work and that she always supported me.

LARGE PROGRAMS MANAGEMENT

I started looking for some other place to work in the company. A friend of mine was part of a group putting together a proposal to build a technical school in Teheran, Iran, and to provide 13 individualized vocational courses to be sent to the school. The Shah had a 25-year economic plan for Iran in which he would make Iran the economic hub of the mid-east. He wanted Iran to move away from oil dependency to the manufacturing of automobiles, electronic devices and other products. To accomplish his goal, he needed people trained in various technical skills. That was where our technical school came into play. Because of my interest in individualized instructions, organizational and writing abilities, I was brought on to help complete the proposal. We succeeded in getting a contract to build one school, with the possibility of several more schools. The eventual plan would be to have up to fifteen schools throughout Iran.

My job was to acquire the thirteen courses, package them to be sent to Iran and to identify all the lab equipment needed for the various courses so they could be acquired and shipped to the school. While I was doing the course-related tasks, others were preparing the school, purchasing equipment, meeting with various Iranian officials, and so on.

About three months into the project, I got a visit from a CDC vice president who wanted to know about the procedures I had written while with my previous organization. He asked specifically if I had written a procedure that identified the requirements for a sale. I told him I had. He asked to see it. We set up to meet at the warehouse. I introduced him to Wayne, the person I had trained to take my place. I told Wayne what we were looking for. He took us to the file cabinet where he had all the procedures. Wayne took out the one we were interested in. It specifically stated that there had to be a Purchase Order number and the Purchase Order had to be signed by a customer representative. A big smile came over his face. He asked if he could take the procedure. Wayne looked in the file of backup copies, found a duplicate which he used to replace the one taken out. Wayne told him he could keep the copy he had. After the VP left, I asked Wayne if he knew what was going on. He said upper management was questioning the legitimacy of the last-minute orders when my previous boss and his sales GM met their quota last year.

A couple of months later, I heard that my procedure had revealed fake Purchase Order numbers on last-minute sales to meet their quota. The sales General Manager was fired and the Vice President was demoted and given 30 days to find a job. He chose to leave the company. *I always felt the Lord's involvement in that whole matter, taking vengeance for me.*

I hired a small staff to package and process course materials as they became available. The courses were being acquired from 916 Vocational Technical school. The school agreed to redo the courses in accordance with our requirements, and to make one set available following an agreed-upon schedule.

I had my staff begin the search for cabinets to house all the material while I met with a group known for their ability to design logos and other graphics to suit a purpose. With the names and descriptions of all thirteen courses in hand, I met with the group and asked if they could design international symbols that would represent each of the thirteen courses. After reading the course titles and descriptions, they said they would have something for me to look at in a month.

A month later I approved the thirteen designs. I got printable originals and they got paid. I took the symbols to a printer and had them reduced and printed on small round sticky labels, about one inch in diameter. They would print sheets of symbols, with a dozen labels on each sheet. We printed hundreds of sheets of each symbol and used them on cabinets and course materials, so students would know which cabinet each item came from. Within each cabinet, zones were set up by shelf, starting with Zone A at the top. Each item was numbered to match the particular place on the shelf that the item belonged. This made it easy for the Iranians to find and return course items.

About six months into the project, my buddy, who was managing the U.S. activities, no longer wanted the job. He recommended me. I was asked if I wanted the job. I told them I did. I was asked if I had a replacement for my current job. I said I did. I got a promotion and my replacement got a promotion.

At this point in time we were training Iranian instructors at 916 who, afterward, would go back to Iran and train other instructors. We were purchasing lab equipment and began staging items at a CDC warehouse in Arden Hills for shipment to Iran. We had people working with Iranian Customs and various workers getting the training building ready.

As the U.S. Program Manager, all operations in the United States related to the Iran Program were under my responsibility. I had 102 people working for me. I had a counterpart working in Iran responsible for all the activities taking place there. I had people working the needs of all 13 courses. I structured the organization so that all equipment needs were funneled through one person who reported directly to me. The contract was a multimillion (U.S. dollars) contract, a large portion of it being spent to acquire courses and equipment to be sent to Iran in accordance with a master schedule.

I knew that we were all in a position of being tempted to accept gifts as a thank you from vendors for our business. I held a staff meeting as soon as I could get all the positions filled. I explained the master plan and timetable we were working toward. I also emphasized that I would not tolerate anyone receiving gifts because of our business. A week later, I arrived at work early, as I usually did, and noticed some boxes in the office next to mine. This was the office of the equipment coordinator. He had told me the previous day that the first part of the equipment purchases would be delivered overnight to his office. I was curious to see what equipment had arrived. On the top of a box in the coordinator's chair was a red crystal digital watch. These were the first digital watches being sold to the public, at ninety dollars and up. I was upset, but left the watch where I found it and returned to my office.

When the coordinator came in I asked him to meet me in my office. I confronted him about the watch. He started to make excuses and I stopped him cold. I told him this was his first warning. I expected him to return the watch and to never receive any other gifts. I asked him if he could do that. He apologized and said it would never happen again. To my knowledge, it never did. I needed this person because when it came to getting items into the country, customs could hold them up indefinitely. I felt he was the perfect guy to "expedite" shipments when needed.

I was away from home a lot during this time and Pam and I began drifting apart. When I was home I spent as much time as I could with everyone, but my absence was having an effect on Pam and the kids. Quite often, when I did come home, Pam would immediately take off on her motorcycle or go to be with her horse. We tried to communicate our concerns about each other, but we were unsuccessful.

We both agreed that we needed to separate for a while. I found a one bedroom furnished apartment and moved in. I would take the kids on weekends whenever I could, giving her time to herself. In a way, this helped me because I could come and go as my job demanded. It was during this time that I had to go to Iran every few weeks and meet with my counterpart. These meetings would give me a better perspective of the problems in Iran.

Before my first trip, my staff that handled the course materials had completed all the courses. They were in cabinets at a staging area in the Arden Hills Control Data facility. I went there personally to manage the handling and packaging of the materials being sent to Iran. I met two people at the Arden Hills facility who would be packaging the materials for shipment. I walked with them throughout the room, showing them what had to be boxed up. I wanted all the cabinets emptied and shipped. The course materials needed to be boxed, using standard cardboard boxes with the CDC logo on them.

To seal the boxes, they had an old tape dispenser that was quite beat up but worked well enough. The dispenser held a roll of wide filament tape with glue on one side. You could adjust the handle swing to cut off the desired length of tape needed. By pulling down on the handle, you forced the tape to pass through a container holding water, to wet the tape, and then the tape was forced against a sharp blade to cut it. The cut tape was then ready to apply to the paper carton to seal it. On the way out, I turned and looked over the whole room and told the two guys that everything in the room had to be boxed up for shipment to Iran. Later, I was told that this course material along with all the equipment and materials for all the courses filled two gutted 707 airplanes when shipped to Iran.

A week later, I was preparing to take my first trip to Iran. I had never flown internationally, so I was a bit apprehensive. Knowing that I had never flown internationally, my boss had his secretary contact each airport I would be flying into and had a customer service representative meet me at the airport. I didn't know this. My first stop was Amsterdam. As soon as I got off the plane and entered the building, I heard someone calling my name. It was a Swissair representative, a beautiful blonde with a nice smile and good English. She escorted me to the terminal where I would catch my next flight. This helped me quite a bit.

It was an hour before my next flight so I sat in a lounge that overlooked part of the runway. I noticed that baggage handlers were unloading an airplane. They were tossing luggage, garment bags and boxes onto the various little luggage carts connected together and pulled by a tractor. As soon as the last item was on the last cart, the tractor driver took off as fast as he could go. On one of the carts, a garment bag had slipped between the cart and a wheel. In no time at all, the garment bag was worn through by the wheel and white pieces of cloth were being thrown all over. The driver continued out of sight oblivious to what was happening behind him. I began to wonder what kind of explanation the airlines would give to the customer whose clothes were ruined.

After clearing customs in Teheran, I was met by an old friend who was working the Iran side of the program. It was great to see a familiar face. I would be staying with him, since he had an extra bedroom. His place was near enough to the school that I could walk, which I did most of the time I was there.

As soon as I entered the school, my counterpart, with sort of a smirk on his face, was eager to tell me that the Iranian Director of the school wanted to see me as soon as I could make it. After greeting several friends and being introduced to Iranians working in and around my counterpart's office, my counterpart and I hastened to the Director's office and where I was introduced by my counterpart. Looking me straight in the face, the Director pulled the old beat-up tape dispenser from behind his chair and placed it on the corner of his desk, and asked what this was. I immediately apologized and told him this was shipped by mistake, and that I would gladly take it off his hands. He said, "No, no," that he would keep it, but was wondering why it was sent. I told him what I had said to the shippers and that they took my words literally when I said to ship everything in the room. He had intended for this to be a one-upsmanship situation, but since I didn't react as he had hoped, he quickly switched subjects.

When I was gone to Iran, Pam could only call me at three to four in the morning her time, because of the ten-hour time difference. All of her calls were primarily about how badly the kids were behaving and how soon would I get back. My first trip lasted two weeks, as planned.

While I was there I had a chance to see how the course materials were being used. The Iranians liked the course icons; it helped to keep materials where they were supposed to be, as intended. There was a full-fledged translation under way of the written material into Farci, the Iranian native language. I showed them various graphic arts techniques to help make their translation easier to understand when there were references to pictures and art contained in the manual. Most of my time, though, was spent in meetings with my counterpart and his staff to resolve various problems between my organization and his. After two weeks, I returned home.

During this time I had moved to a BSF group closer to home, as did Doug Hansen. It was in a large Evangelical Free Church, whose pastor was pleased to have the church facilities available to the group. BSF met in the basement. The size of this group was about 180 men. At the first group meeting, the pastor came down, and at the meeting of the full group, gave a welcome to everyone and expressed his sincere pleasure of having the men's BSF group meet in the church. I met him this first evening and made an appointment to meet with him during the week.

I still had not found a church to be going to and, since I was a bit familiar with this church, I wanted to inquire about what requirements and beliefs members had to agree to. I met the pastor the following Saturday morning at his office in the church. He wanted to know my religious background, which I told him. He then explained that the main requirement was belief as given in the Apostles Creed. I was familiar with that and already believed all of it. Baptism was a requirement to become an active member of the church; the Baptism could be either infant or adult. I was pleased with what I heard. We talked about various activities that the church held. Knowing that I was in BSF, he expressed, again, his pleasure having the group meet in the church.

He asked me who it was that brought me to Jesus and my belief in God. I told him that I had always believed in God. I thought a bit about Jesus in my life and realized my relationship with Jesus had grown through my personal Bible Studies. When I told him that, he sort of marveled. He was expecting me to name some individual as being responsible.

I began going to this church every Sunday that I could. Pam accompanied me once in a while but she was not too motivated about church. She never complained about me attending, however, and I always thanked God for that.

Pam and I began having discussions concerning our differences. In her free time she was spending more and more time with a single male neighbor. I heard about it from the kids and neighbors. I confronted her with it. She said he was just a friend and someone for her to talk to. She wanted me to spend more time with her and the kids. She was trying to control my life and I wanted her to stop. Our discussion went on and on. No arguments or condemnations, just facts and concerns. It was our best discussion to date. She invited me to dinner that Friday evening, I could take the kids after the meal.

The meal went well. She and I agreed to write down all of our concerns and to have a face-to-face meeting to see if we could resolve our differences. A few days later, we worked out our differences and made agreements to resolve all of our issues. We decided to get back together after my next trip, and give the marriage one more try. It was now time for me to make another trip to Iran. I had decided that this would be my last trip, since my work was part of our problem. When I got back I would find a different job.

This trip to Iran was much more work-oriented. We had our meetings and resolved differences, but there was a problem that no one had addressed. How were the Iranians going to train instructors how to teach? They asked me if I could do a Train the Trainer course and also teach how to develop training materials. I put together a trainer course and taught some basics of presentation techniques. I also wrote a course on the techniques of course development, which I drafted and turned over to their staff. All of this extra work was extending my stay there, but I felt I had to do it so my need to return would be diminished. Pam and I talked frequently. She was in a more cheerful mood since she and I planned to get back together. She was disappointed about my two-week extension, but she understood my reasoning.

The Friday evening before my flight to the U.S. the next day, a friend of mine working in Iran wanted to take me to an American restaurant in downtown Teheran for a steak dinner. He and I sat at a booth with a large window overlooking the sidewalk and street outside. We had placed our orders and were enjoying each other's company when a young Iranian man walked by the window, turned around and looked at us. He then started shouting and raising his fist as in defiance as he walked away. The two of us looked at each other and shrugged our shoulders, not knowing what that was all about. I returned to the U.S. the next day. That same day, the U.S. embassy was taken over by Iranian students.[5] This brought the entire program to a halt. I would not have to go back to Iran after all.

SMALL FARMER PROGRAM

Following the Iran Program, I joined a group of people within CDC whose mission was to bring technology to small farmers. This was a pet project of Control Data's CEO. He had been a small farmer when he was growing up and wanted to do what he could to help them compete with large, commercial farmers. He was given an annual five million dollar budget to be used as he saw fit. This was our budget to help the small farmers. My boss, General Manager for the project, would provide a verbal progress report directly to the CEO on a monthly basis.

The group was divided into three areas: Instructional programs, an informational data base, and business technology. I was assigned the instructional programs area with the task of going around the country and contracting with colleges and universities and acquiring self-teach courses related to all areas of farming. While I was doing that, one of my peers was to develop a computer data base helpful to farmers that would be collected from all over the world, and the other of my peers was to develop business-related software that would help farmers manage their farms.

SECOND HOUSE

Pam and I decided to begin looking for a second house. We wanted something closer in to the cities and easier driving distance to work and stores. We ended up having a four-bedroom house built in Eden Prairie. During its construction, Pam and I would visit often to monitor the progress.

Pam and I had two cars at this time. For some reason, I don't remember why, we were taking both cars. We were going to check on the progress of the Eden Prairie house and Pam was directly behind me when I entered an intersection and a garbage truck came down a hill to my left, too fast into the intersection and couldn't stop. I saw the truck out of the corner of my eye and slammed on my brakes. The truck cut off my car's driver-side front fender, shearing it like a knife blade. Had I not slowed down, the vehicle would have hit the driver's side door. *God's hand in my life.*

We exchanged information with the garbage truck driver. After the police wrote up an accident report, and got a tow for my car, I called my insurance company to report the accident and then we continued to the house. We were meeting the builder to go over some last minute details about the house and didn't want to miss the meeting.

Soon after, we moved into the new house on a cul de sac. It was a great 3-level house with four bedrooms and two baths up, Half Bath, Kitchen, Dining Room, Living Room (with fireplace) and Den on the main level, and unfinished basement with a second fireplace. I later finished an Office, Family Room, Bed Room, Bathroom and Laundry

Room in the basement. It was an ideal home for us at this time in our lives, giving everyone more living space and room to entertain, as needed.

I was traveling a lot at this time because of my work. My job took me to higher educational institutions all over the U.S. We had identified 30 areas of instruction and I was to find these courses and make them available to farmers in a self-teach format. We wanted to rely heavily on audio and video as well as text. We also wanted the courses to be easy for the farmers to use. At this time, the 3M Company, working with Philips, developed a video disc that could be used for motion or still images, along with accompanying voice recording, much like what we wanted to do with the 16mm projector years before. At this time, the video disc was 10 inches in diameter and would hold about two hours of material. This was a predecessor to current CDs and DVDs. It was easy to use and eliminated the need for a separate slide projector and video projector. The only problem was that the disc player weighed about 30 pounds!

Within two years, I was able to reach my goal of 30 courses and get them into a self-teach format, all within my allotted budget. To make it easy for farmers to use the courses, I modified the learning carrels we had developed for the City University of New York to accommodate the video disc and cassettes. We had 10 farmers in Minnesota who agreed to be test farmers for our project. We would give them the courses free and they would provide detailed critiques of the courses so we could improve upon them before going national.

I acquired space in downtown Princeton, Minnesota, for a pilot project to house the courses, learning carrel, and office space for a full-time librarian who would interface and assist farmers, as necessary. We had courses on pigs, beef cattle, dairy cattle, and sheep, along with courses on a variety of crops. In our second year, when testing was still underway, I had achieved all my goals and was under budget, compared with my two peers who had gone over budget and not met all their goals. My boss said he had a Director position open up in the group and I was one of two candidates for the promotion. This was the promotion I was waiting for. Director was the lowest executive position in the company. From there one could advance to General Manager and then Vice Presidency. With my record, I was confident I would get the promotion. At BSF, I told Doug Hansen of my pending promotion so he had the whole group praying for me.

A few days later I was called into my boss' office and told he had made his decision and gave the promotion to my peer. I was dumbfounded. He assured me that my performance was excellent; however my peer had saved my boss when he was out of a job a few years back, so he felt obligated to return the favor. I was angry and went home. I told Pam what had happened. She tried to console me, but I was too angry. After I calmed down a bit, I went into the bedroom, closed the door and prayed to God for understanding. There was no understanding coming forth.

I went to work for the next two weeks, after which time my boss called me into his office and told me my job was being taken over by the peer who had just been promoted. My boss gave me a year to find a job in the company. I would continue on full salary but I should not come in to the office. I was to call him weekly with my progress in finding a job. This astounded me. Now I was totally confused with what was happening in my life. First no promotion and now no job! *In reflection concerning this matter, God was involved: A year to find a job and still at full salary!*

I cleaned out my desk and drove slowly home, contemplating the recent events in my life. What was happening? I told Pam the bad news. This time she was not as understanding and became angry as well. This didn't help. I went into the bedroom again and prayed for understanding, but none came. At BSF, the group was praying for me. Doug and I continued our prayer breakfasts. He was a great help to me at this time. He was sure that I would get an answer when the time was right.

I went to CDC nearly every day at first, to an area set up to help people find jobs within the company. At any given time, there were 50 or more people using this facility. There was a small staff there who helped with resumes, provided an active list of jobs available, had private offices with phones for our use and provided clerical and answering services. I called my boss weekly and gave him my progress report. Weeks and then months went by, with no job prospects. I was beginning to get concerned and continued praying for guidance and understanding.

One time when I was praying, a terrible feeling of guilt and shame came over me. I reflected on my work life and realized that God had been behind every one of my promotions and I had been taking the credit. I begged his forgiveness and at that moment I realized, I think for the first time, that He is sovereign and can do whatever He wants. I don't have any right to even question why things happen. I wept, thinking how foolish I had been to demand an explanation from Him.

I only had two weeks to go with my job searching before my year would be up. There had been no job prospects at all either in the company or outside. When I went in to CDC that day, I received a call from George, who was heading up a small CDC function with the task of providing multimedia courses to colleges. My name had come up, so he called me. I met with George and by the end of the day, I had a job. *As I said before, God may not be early, but He is never late.*

I have reflected on this period of my life many times since. Even when I was angry and demanding of God, He took care of me. I went nearly a whole year with full pay while I was looking for a job. Why so long; and why full pay? When I was ready, God revealed His reason for what had happened; which was that I needed to recognize that He was my reason for success, and that He was sovereign. I had not recognized what that really meant until then. I do not think anything less than what happened to me would have opened my eyes. Furthermore, I firmly believe that had I gotten the promotion to Director, I would probably have gone on to Vice Presidency and would have turned away from God and Pamela. The money and associated luxuries would have been my idols. I have thanked Him many times for not giving up on me.

MULTI-MEDIA PRODUCTS

The little group, headed by George, consisted of him, me and a secretary. It was one of the few areas of the company making a profit. Business had expanded to the point where he needed help; that's where I came in. George had acquired a large inventory of multimedia courses, primarily on fundamental subjects like basic math and English as a second language. Colleges were dealing with a lot of incoming students graduating from high school who could not pass their entrance exam. They wanted to provide such basic courses in a self-teach format so that prospective students could learn required basic knowledge to pass the entrance exam without burdening the college staff. That's where our courses came in.

George took me to the distribution center that kept our inventory and shipped out our orders. Lo and behold, Wayne, whom I had trained years ago, was still in charge of distribution, only it had grown very large with the addition of multimedia courses. We were glad to see each other after so many years. Wayne gave us a tour of his facility and showed us the multimedia courses, packaged in cabinets like we had done on the Iran program.

We produced advertising brochures of the various courses and sent these out to colleges and universities. In most cases, orders came from the mailings, but once in a while a visit to a college or university was needed to close a sale. Whenever the need came up, I would usually travel to make the deal.

1987

1987 was not a good year for Pam and me. On April 23 of that year, we lost our 21-year-old son, Michael, to an accident. He had decided to become a Christian Counselor. He had completed three years of college and was taking time off from school to save money for his last year. He worked at Perkins Restaurant in Minnetonka as an evening cook. Pam and I had a spare car (a Toyota) that we provided to Michael and his sister, Sally, to share. It was between them who had the car on a given day. On this particular day, they had a disagreement. Michael was angry and took off for work on his bicycle. It was light out so he had no problem peddling the few miles to work.

When it came time for Michael to get off work, however, it was dark. Sally drove to the restaurant to give him a ride home. The bicycle would not fit in the small car and Michael did not want to leave it at the restaurant, so he began bicycling home in the dark. Highway 101, a narrow road at the time, had a very sharp turn in it. Whether Michael was crossing over at that point or the driver of a car was too far over, at the turn, Michael was hit by the car and died at the scene. Pam and I were notified by the police to go to a hospital; that our son had been involved in an accident.

Pam and I feared the worse as we drove to the hospital. It was one of the most horrible experiences I ever had. I saw him dead but could not believe it. I was in shock, as was Pam. This was another time when I could not understand why this had happened. He had turned his life over to Jesus, was liked by his friends, was already doing counseling with many of them and was just starting his adult life. I wrestled with why for many months.

In BSF I had a desire to meet a Jewish person. I thought it would be nice to get their perspective of the Bible and Jesus. I had prayed and forgot about it. As it turned out, the person who hit Michael with his car was a Jewish doctor, a Psychiatrist I believe. He contacted the police and asked if he could come to the viewing. They passed on the request to the funeral home where we were at. The funeral home people passed on the request to me and Pam. They also highly recommended that we do not meet him. I felt otherwise and said he could come and I would talk with him.

He came expressing his deepest sympathy. He wanted to talk, so he and I went into a private room and talked for half an hour. He could not understand why I didn't have bitterness toward him. I asked him if he knew Jesus; he said he did not know who that was. I proceeded to give him a short overview of Jesus' life and why I believed as I did. I felt the Holy Spirit with me as I talked. We parted on good terms. I never saw or heard from him again, but I believe God had a purpose in our meeting, and I had met a Jew as I had prayed.

Following Michael's death, I had been away from work for two weeks when I got a call asking when I would be back; things were piling up. I went to work but Pam was so badly affected by Michael's death, she could not be out of my presence for very long. We made arrangements for her to be with me at work. Friends stopped by to give their condolences, but not knowing what to say. It was a very unusual time. Eventually, Pam was able to function in my absence, and life began to return to being more normal.

I began working harder and longer as a way of coping. I prayed a lot and still could not understand why Michael died.

One good thing during this time was our grandson Jonathan's birth on April 19, four days before Michael's death. Mike had a chance to hold Jonathan. His face seemed to be in amazement as he held the tiny infant in his arms. It almost seemed like God's timing was to help reduce our grief by bringing Jonathan into our lives at this time.

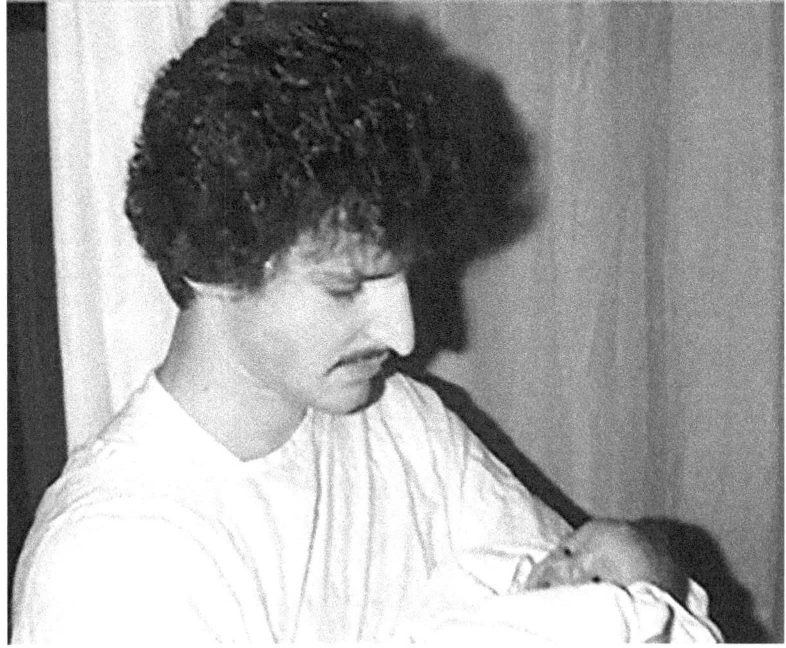

Figure 9. Michael Holding Jonathan

Prior to Jonathan's birth, my daughter Joan had moved back into our house. I had talked to the father when Joan was first pregnant, to see if he was going to be a responsible person. He told me he would be glad to play his father role if I let him live with us at no cost to him. I was in shock that he would have such an attitude. Following that, Pam and I decided to take on the responsibility of raising Jonathan. Joan would pay what she could toward his costs.

On July 23 of that year we had what they called a 100 year storm. Our house sat near the top of a hill. There was a sump in the basement to drain off any water buildup. I never got a pump for the sump because we had never needed it. What little water came in would quickly drain out to a lower drain field in our back yard. That evening Pam's mother had gone to the basement and hurried back up to tell Pam and I that there was water in the basement. We went down to find my office and the family room in three inches of water. We pulled carpeting and mopped the floors with several towels, wringing them outside the patio door. The sump drain was now getting ahead of the incoming water and in an hour or so the water was no longer coming into the house.

We turned the carpeting over onto boxes, exposing the wet bottom. We set up several fans, blowing onto the carpeting. We were able to save the carpeting, but we both noted that it happened on the 23rd.

On September 23 of that same year, I was called into a vice president's office to be informed that they were closing down our operation and that George and I and the secretary were out of jobs. The vice president knew I had recently lost my son and, after telling me of the operation closure, said: "You're not going to do anything foolish are you?" I wasn't sure what he meant by the question, but I was still not very clear-minded from Michael's death. By the end of that day, I was no longer an employee of CDC, after 24 years of service. My severance pay was substantial, so there wouldn't be any immediate concerns about income.

I created a business, called Carney Associates, to provide services to industry in Training and Development, Publishing, and Program Management.

Carney Associates (1987-2000)

Because of my knowledge and experience at CDC, and as a hobby, I had been doing a lot of work with desktop publishing, so I prepared business cards, made a portfolio of my capabilities and began calling on companies. It was not long before I had work coming in. It wasn't enough to meet all our bills, but it was a start.

I was continuing in BSF and got to know a lot of the other leaders. I was always amazed that there were 180 men who chose to get together Monday evenings to study the Bible. Even more amazing to me was that this was only one of several other BSF groups in the state, and many, many more throughout the country. It was nondenominational, so a small study group might have participants from different denominations. This added depth to the discussions and was never a problem except one time when there were two people in my group from different Lutheran denominations. They had some disagreements, but it never got emotional.

A person could continue in BSF for five years. Each year the study took a different part of the Bible. Participants were encouraged to use their own Bible; however, the studies used The King James Bible. If someone wanted to acquire a Bible, the King James was recommended simply to align with the study references. After five years, participants could not continue in BSF unless they opted to be a leader. This allowed an influx of new participants every year.

Each week, participants were given worksheets that covered the material to be studied. By filling in blanks or answering questions in the worksheets, a participant was prepared for the next meeting. At the meeting, the entire group would assemble, and then following announcements, the group would break up into smaller groups of ten to twenty. Participants were assigned to the smaller group so that the same people would meet throughout the Bible Study Period.

I was now a leader in BSF, for the first time. Leaders went to a retreat where they prepared for the upcoming year's bible study. During that retreat, some of the people from the BSF headquarters in San Antonio, Texas, did a one-day bible study for the leaders, as a form of inspiration. This year, their topic was the book of Job. It was this study that opened my eyes to the fact that God allows bad things to happen to people for a greater good. The suffering of Job was to make him a better person; and, at the end, it was his prayers for his wayward friends that God accepts. Job is also rewarded beyond what he had lost.

I thought about that and realized that God had to have taken Michael for a reason. It didn't matter whether I knew the reason; it was His choice to make. That night I was no longer angry with God but, instead, thankful that in his infinite wisdom He took Mike and it had to be for a good reason. I finally had peace about everything that was happening to me. I went home that night confident that God had a plan for my future. I just had to do my part.

Each small group had a leader who would conduct the Bible Study. Following the small group study, everyone reassembled for a summary by the overall BSF leader. Although it seemed to have been frowned on by Headquarters BSF Management, our BSF group would have a small group leader give a short testimonial each week prior to the leader's summary. To me this was the most powerful part of the evening. It was not uncommon for participants to seek out the person giving the testimonial and thank him because it touched them in some way.

At my first year as a leader at BSF, I led a group of twelve men. One of the men in the group was an older man confined to a wheelchair. He had been in BSF the previous year and had been disruptive of the class, as I found out later. Being an experienced instructor helped me handle this person. He tried several times to dominate the discussion and to bring it away from the topic we were supposed to discuss. I would not let him dominate and maintained control. We were able to get through the material in spite of his distractions.

After a couple weeks of this person's distractions, I mentioned to the BSF upper management that this person should not be in BSF. He didn't study his lesson and he was bringing up irrelevant things to discuss that were a disservice to the rest of the people in the class. Their reply was that "We can't discriminate against anyone who wants to be in BSF."

I prayed to God about it and left it with that. This person would call me at various times for me to give him a ride somewhere. I would accommodate if I could; whenever I did so, Pam came along as well.

I mentioned all this to Doug Hansen. He knew of the guy and had talked to his Baptist friend about it. The next Friday I got a call from Doug who said that he and his friend were going to have a breakfast with the guy from my class the next morning and wanted me to be there. His friend said they were going to "Test the Spirit." I wasn't sure what that meant, but I was interested and said I'd be there.

Doug, I and his friend had agreed to meet a few minutes before they had the other person join us. Doug's friend wanted to inform me what was going to happen. Doug's friend said that they were going to test the spirit of this individual who was so disruptive in my BSF class. He explained that 1 John tells how to test the spirit, and he read the following from his Bible:

> 1John 4:1*: Beloved, believe not every spirit, but try the spirits whether they are of God: because many false prophets are gone out into the world. 4:2 Hereby know ye the Spirit of God: Every spirit that confesseth that Jesus Christ is come in the flesh is of God: 4:3 And every spirit that confesseth not that Jesus Christ is come in the flesh is not of God: and this is that spirit of antichrist, whereof ye have heard that it should come; and even now already is it in the world.*

The individual came a few minutes later. We all had breakfast (Doug's friend was paying) and did a lot of chit chat until we were all done with the meal. At this time Doug's friend asked the disruptive guy if he believed in God. The man said he did. He was then asked if he believed in Jesus Christ. The man hemmed and hawed. Said he believed he was a great man and all that. He was then asked point blank if he believed that Jesus Christ was the son of God. The man flatly denied it. I was astounded. After the man left, we talked a bit. Doug's friend said that anyone with an evil spirit cannot admit that Jesus is the son of God. That's the test of the spirit.

After about 4 or 5 weeks into BSF, this person had to leave the class to have a bowel movement. He had requested that his personal assistant (a female nurse) be allowed to attend BSF. This was denied; since this group was only for men (there were also female BSF groups). He had problems getting his clothes down and transferring to the toilet. He yelled for help. One of the standby managers went and found that the man had gone all over the floor and himself. It took a lot of time to clean him and the mess up. This manager was beside himself and insisted that the person no longer be part of this group. They found out that he had moved out of the area, found the BSF group that was in that area, then confronted the man saying he could not attend our BSF group because of his move, but that there was a group in his new area. They gave him the BSF contact and told him he could not attend BSF here anymore. *The Lord took care of the problem.* I never heard from or saw the man again.

During a monthly get-together of people looking for work, I went and saw several people who had done work for me at various times when I was at CDC. In one case, a gal had interviewed for a temporary opening at Honeywell. She felt she was not qualified; however, I might be, since they were looking for someone with training development capability. She gave me the number to call. As it turned out, the facility was moving to a new location and would require the development of training courses for their 600 employees. I went in for an interview and got the job on the spot. When it came to my salary, I said $40 an hour. The person interviewing me said, "Why should I pay you $40 an hour?" I looked him straight in the eyes and said, "Because I am worth it." He told me later, that was why he hired me. He was looking for someone with confidence to do this tremendous job.

HONEYWELL (1988-1989)

The job was initially for six months. Because we achieved all our goals and exceeded them in some cases, my contract was extended another six months to give time for additional training and development needed. This gave me the opportunity to help set up a graphics production function to produce training materials in house. I also provided a Train-the-Trainer course for the various managers within the facility. None of these had ever done training, but were now required to do so as part of their job.

There was a group of people responsible for various portions of the transfer. Their weekly meeting would identify problems early and devote the necessary resources to solving the problem. The head of this group reported directly to Honeywell upper management. It was an excellent method of keeping things on track.

This year with Honeywell was the highest salary I ever earned in a single year. It also provided me with experiences and capabilities that I would use later on. *God's hand in my life.*

About this time, my grandson, Jonathan, got very sick. I can remember Pam bringing Jonathan to me shouting: "He has stopped breathing!" She got on the phone to call an ambulance while I went in to the living room, praying to God for help. In my frustration, I raised Jonathan with both hands toward the ceiling and cried out: "Not again, please, Lord!" At that very instant, Jonathan began breathing. He had turned blue and now his face was back to a normal color. When Pam came in from her call, I told her the good news and passed Jonathan back to her. What a relief! The emergency people came, looked Jonathan over and advised that he be taken to his regular doctor for his bad cough. We took him and discovered that Jonathan had the croup. He eventually got over that as well. *God's hand in my life.*

Before I left Honeywell, I picked up publishing jobs from several departments; one being a monthly newsletter. These and other jobs provided income for a while; but as time went on, I was back taking in less than our bills.

In late December of 1989, I began to get sweats and chest pains. I couldn't walk very far without running out of breath. That Sunday I went to a church I had been going to for a while. After the service I asked to be prayed on for my health condition. A lady at the church was gifted in prayer. She and two other church members came over to me. The lady placed her hand on my heart and began praying in a tongue I had never heard before. After a few minutes she asked if I felt anything. I told her I did not. She did this three times. On the third time, I felt a warm feeling around my heart and she stopped praying. I have since learned that this warmth is the presence of the Holy Spirit.

The following Tuesday I saw my doctor who said I had classic signs of angina. This was the first week of January 1990; I was admitted to the hospital. On Wednesday, when they checked my arteries for blockages, they found three arteries had problems; one of those was an artery that feeds two-thirds of the heart. It was 95% closed. They immediately stopped the test because the extra stress could cause a heart attack at any time. They placed me in intensive care. The doctor who would do the surgery was on vacation and would be available the next day to do the operation. They asked if I wanted to wait a day. I remembered that warmth from the Holy Spirit and agreed to the delay. The doctor would certainly be well-rested. That Thursday I had a triple bypass operation.

I remember the surgeon who had done my operation had a "Secretary" who was beautiful. The first time I saw her, Pam was there and we were talking. This gorgeous woman walks up to my bed, in a nurse's outfit, but wearing high heels and with beautiful long fingernails, introduces herself and said she wanted to take my vitals. As soon as she touched my chest with her stethoscope, my heart did a double-beat and I gasped. She and Pam both noticed my reaction, Pam laughed and the nurse just smiled. I got the feeling that this reaction from her patients was not new. Although this "Secretary" looked out of place, she was highly respected and excellent at her job.

After a few days of recovery, I was home again. *God's hand in my life.*

SELLING HOUSE (1993-1994)

It was at this point in time that Pam and I decided to sell the house and move to a less expensive one. She wanted a place for horses and I wanted a workshop where I could continue working on cedar chests in my leisure time. We wanted to find a house we could buy outright with the equity in our current home.

Selling the house became a difficult task. After listing with a realtor and preparing the house for sale, we had the added intrusion into our lives of having to take ourselves, along with a cat and dog, out for a drive every time a realtor wanted to show the house, even though the showings failed to produce a single buyer. After months of disruptions in our lives, Pam and I needed a break. We told the realtor we were taking a vacation and the house was off the market until we got back.

It was November, 1993, Pam and I drove to Denver, Colorado. She had never been there, and I wanted to see the city and mountains once again. I thought it would make an interesting way of celebrating our upcoming 30th anniversary. Our timing was pretty good. We only had one delay on the way because of snow. When we got there, we found a motel on the outskirts of Denver and spent each day sightseeing. It was just the thing we needed to get our minds off selling the house; however, we still had problems with realtors bringing in customers against our orders and daughter Joan's (who was staying in the house while we were gone).

Pam and I had brought along dress-up clothes for our anniversary. We were going to go to a fancy restaurant. When the time came, she looked at me and asked: "Do you want to dress up?" Knowing she really didn't want to get dressed up, I answered "No." She was pleased. We still went out and enjoyed a nice dinner, but without the change of clothes.

Earlier in our marriage, Pam enjoyed dressing up and going out. During the first five years of our marriage with three young children, we couldn't afford to go out. When Pam's mother moved in and my income had increased, the opportunity for us to go out presented itself and we took it, gladly.

As for me, I had worn a uniform or a suit since the time I went into the service. When I retired, I put away my suit and wore only casual clothes or denims. It felt like I was removing a burden.

After the trip, when we got back to the house, we had a meeting with the realtor, who apologized for other realtors not heeding our wishes. He advised us to replace the carpeting, to make the house more appealing. He also said we should put up a natural Christmas tree, which he would provide free. This, he said, provided a better attraction than an artificial tree.

We got the carpet replaced and put up a natural Christmas tree, and brought the house back on the market. This time we did not go out of the house when the house was shown. We all gathered in the living room reading or watching TV. There were not many showings in December, but January had several, including a couple who had seen the house before. Apparently, the realtor was right about the carpeting because the couple ended up making a bid on the house, which we liked. The problem now was that we had not found a place to move to.

We knew we had to sell the house regardless, so we picked a closing date in February.

Within days of setting the closing date, we found a hobby farm that was just what we wanted and could close on it a couple days after the closing date of the house. The buyers of our house could not move in immediately and allowed us to move out after closing on the new house. *With God's hand involved in all this*, the move went like clockwork. We were able to pay for the house outright and still had money to buy horses and make necessary improvements.

RUSH CITY HOME (1994)

It took two trips in a rented 26-foot van to haul all of our belonging to the new house. Doug Hansen helped with the move. It was about two below zero by the time we had the truck emptied the first day. Doug stayed overnight and helped with the move the next day.

It was an old house with one level above ground and a full basement. It had a wood stove in the basement but we were using the old propane furnace at the beginning. I had the previous owners leave a load of split wood, which I planned to burn when I got around to it. About a week after we moved in, I fired up the wood stove for the first time. It was overheating the house at first because I wasn't used to the damper settings. After a week or so, I was getting the burning rate and heat at the proper levels. After two weeks we only used the propane furnace to keep the chill off at night. Eventually we only burned wood during the winter and never used the propane furnace after that.

In the spring of our first year in the house, we bought two horses and had them trained. We cleared areas and put in a pasture for the horses. It was a lot of work but we were up to the task. It was interesting when we put in the fence for the pasture. I had seen how some farmer fences were built; they had wooden posts within long runs and at every corner. The posts consisted of one vertical and an angled post attached to each side of the vertical, along the direction of the fence. The vertical posts required holes dug in the ground with a post-hole digger. As it turned out, Pam was good at post-hole digging, so she dug all the post holes while I put in all the metal posts, every eight feet between the wooden posts. The wooden posts absorbed the tension when the wiring for the fence was tightened.

We spent three weeks putting in the fence. When we were done, we had a pasture that fenced in all the usable land in the back and sides of our property. We also had a 16' by 24' Loafing Shed built for the horses. For electricity in the shed, I ran an underground wire from the garage to the shed and installed an overhead light with a switch, and several outlets. After the fence was installed, I ran two runs of barbed wire along the fence; one a quarter way up from the ground and the other at the middle. Last of all I ran a regular metal wire near the top of the fence and connected it to an electric pulser. I had the pulser installed in the large shed that came with the house. This would keep the horses from trying to go over the fence. It worked great.

The horses were delivered to us about a month after their purchase. It was great having them in the pasture. It was a mother-daughter pair, which had never been separated. They looked so good in the pasture. After a while we could whistle or yell and they would come running to us, especially at feeding time. I bought bales of hay from a farmer, twenty-five at a time, loaded on the back of my pickup and a 4 x 8 foot trailer hooked to the back of the truck. The bales were stored in the back of the large shed where we parked the van.

We bought a saddle and blanket for Pam as well as a bridle and other necessary items for her to ride the horses. About two weeks after we got the horses, Pam decided to ride the daughter. I had installed a hitching post outside the fenced area between the shed and the garage. She got all the items on the horse to ride and led the horse to the driveway, where I was waiting. I held the horse while she got on. As soon as I released the horse for Pam to ride, the horse bucked her off. Pam hit the gravel driveway with her right shoulder and head while the horse took off for Highway 61, a main highway that went by our home.

I was in a panic but decided that Pam's situation was more important than trying to get the horse back. Pam stood up and was very shaken by the experience. We looked at highway 61 and the horse had turned around and was going past our house. Our neighbor had seen what had happened, caught the horse and led her to me. We opened the gate to the pasture and she ran in to her mother. I took Pam to the clinic to have her checked out. She had a concussion, but was otherwise fine. She never rode a horse again. We now had two expensive pets, which we kept for a couple of years and then sold. Incidentally, I never got my workshop (sigh).

During this period of time I was doing publishing jobs for various businesses and spending much of my free time at home processing wood. Each year I would do six or seven cords of firewood for our stove. This was the heat for our house in the winter. There was a wood stove in our basement with a grate in the floor above the stove. The grate had a fan to bring up the heat from below into the main part of the house. After a few years I was able to maintain a comfortable temperature in the house throughout the winter. Wood was cheap, but it required a lot of labor. I would have logs delivered, then I would cut into rounds, split the rounds, pile the split wood for drying and, when needed, bring in the wood to a wood room I had in the basement. Compared to propane heat, the wood cut our fuel bill by 60 per cent.

I enjoyed all this hard labor. It kind of reminded me of working with wood when we first moved into the big house in Mars Hill, so many years ago

GRAND CASINO PROJECT (1996-1997)

A couple of years after we settled in the house, I got a call from an old CDC friend of mine who had gone into business. The Grand Casino was building a second casino in Hinckley, Minnesota, and needed the development of 21 training programs. My friend was coordinating different aspects of the programs and was looking for someone with publishing experience to do the training manuals. I met with him and we agreed upon an hourly rate for me to do the first manual. If I could produce the manual within his estimated cost, I would go on to do all the other manuals.

At the time, I did not have the software needed to do the manual with my home computer, so I had to go to his home and do the manual there. I received handwritten copy, which I typed and formatted into a draft manual for review and final edit. I designed the manual format, which was approved, and then typed in the text. Where line art was required, I did that also. Photographs, provided by the customer, were resized as necessary, captioned, and then inserted into the draft. The final draft was reviewed and approved with marked-up changes. When I completed the manual, it was ready to be printed.

The first manual was completed in less time and lower cost than my friend had budgeted; as a result, I got the contract to complete all the remaining manuals. By about the third or fourth manual, I had acquired a new computer and the necessary software to do everything needed at home. I was also able to give my friend a quote to do each of the following manuals, based upon his input. This made it easier for both of us. He didn't have to worry about how many hours it would take, and I was confident that I could get the manuals done within the cost figures.

The Grand Casino project lasted two years and provided a good source of income. Meanwhile I was also doing other desktop publishing jobs when I met a person who needed a manual done for a course he would be presenting at a Technical College. In various conversations with this person, I mentioned the training program I had helped develop at Honeywell, related to policies and procedures. He suggested I get the course together and approach the college because they were desperate to find training programs to help companies improve quality standards. There was a big push throughout industry for companies to meet certain quality standards; if they did, their products and services would be more attractive to customers than the products and services of companies that did not meet those standards.

TEACHING AT LOCAL COLLEGES (1997-2000)

In my spare time I began developing a student manual for the Policies and Procedures course. When I got most of it in draft form, I pulled out the Table of Contents and some graphics I would use in the course and made a proposal to a Technical College to teach the course for them to business students. They accepted the proposal. We agreed upon a fee. They would do all the advertising, provide a training room, take care of necessary amenities, such as coffee, rolls and lunch while I provided copies of manuals and did the teaching.

This went well for a while, but it seemed that the college was not making much of an effort to get students. We needed to have three students for the course to break even. After the needed three students, I needed two students to cover my costs. At first, we had 15 to 20 students, so I was making a good amount in teaching the course, but as time went on, the attendance dwindled to less than ten students.

At this time I got a call from a person at another Technical College who had seen the advertising from the first Technical College. He said he would like to know more about the course and suggested that I might teach it in their school as well. We met and agreed for me to teach the course. I told him my concerns with first Technical College not being very aggressive in promoting the course. He said he would promote the course and I would decide whether there were enough students to have the seminar. In addition, they would give me the entire tuition and they would print the student manuals. They were really interested in showing the public that they were providing a solution to their quality problem. That meant more to them than the tuition from my course.

I began teaching at the second Technical College and, in time, stopped teaching at the first. The second Technical College did a better job of promoting the course and even set up seminars to be taught at customer sites. I was asked if I could develop a Flow Charting course as a tool for use in procedures. I developed the course and began teaching that at the Technical College, as well.

The teaching went on for several years. I wanted to retire when I turned 65, only a couple years away. I approached the college with a proposal for them to buy my course so that they could continue teaching it after I retired. I would train their instructor and provide masters of all the training materials. I would give them a non-exclusive agreement to use my materials. They could pay the amount I asked for in a lump sum or in several payments. The initial response was that they would do it.

When I told Pam, she was happy because she could now buy a new car. On the basis of the college interest in acquiring the course, we went out and bought our big van. It turned out that the school changed their mind so now we had an expensive van to pay for. As a result, we got a loan from the bank based on the equity in the house. We paid off the van because the bank payments were lower than the van payments.

Retirement (2000-2017)

I retired in year 2000 at the age of 65. At first we were able to live on my Social Security and retirement checks. However, Pam was not retired yet, and her medical premiums were increasing substantially each year.

MEDICAL PROBLEMS (2002)

I had been having stomach problems for several days. I went to the doctor, but nothing was found. After a couple of weeks, I developed a pain in my right side. If I had been younger, my doctor would have suspected appendicitis. Again nothing was found so the doctor sent me to the hospital for evaluation and more tests. The doctor at the hospital concluded that I had appendicitis. He bragged about a less-invasive way of removing the appendix, which had minimal scarring. With all the scars from my previous heart surgery, another scar didn't matter to me. I underwent surgery the next day. The doctor said that when they went in to remove the appendix, it had already burst. They didn't know how I remained alive because it had burst some time before I got to the hospital! I was to remain in the hospital overnight and be released the next day. *God's hand in my life.*

About 7 p.m. I felt the strongest abdominal pain I had ever felt in my life. I was screaming at the top of my lungs, the pain was so bad. They told me to quiet down, which was impossible for me; they sedated me. When I woke up I was told that following the appendectomy, the doctor had not sewn the cut completely and I had bled internally. The sharp pain was my blood touching some of my internal organs (they said that blood is caustic concerning raw flesh.) They said I had lost half of my blood and was given seven pints of blood to replace what I had lost. I had had a heart attack in the process so I was being transferred to the University Medical Center to take care of my heart.

At the university hospital, doctors discovered that my heart had arrhythmia, but the pooled blood had to take priority. They found that the replacement blood I had been given was tainted with e-coli and streptococci. I was given a heavy dosage of antibiotics and, after several days hoping that the body would absorb the blood and realizing it would take a very long time, they decided to begin pumping out the pooled blood. When they were able to run tests, they found that my heart valve was 96% closed. They stopped the test because I could have another heart attack at any time. They had looked at two of my stints from my first heart surgery twelve years ago. They couldn't understand it, but the stints were as fresh and clean as the day they were put in. *God's hand in my life.*

The operation went well. I now had a porcine valve. After a few days, I was released; I had been in the University Hospital a total of 38 days!

Another evidence of God's hand in all of this: My brother, Dennis, was visiting from California. He arrived before I went to the hospital. He had planned to stay a couple of weeks. When I went into the hospital for the long stay, he took care of all the yardwork. He enjoyed the work and I didn't have to worry about hiring someone to do it. When we found out I would be in the hospital for a longer time, Dennis volunteered to stay until I was back home again.

He said that the exercise had been good for him. Although I had a riding lawnmower, which he used at the beginning, Dennis began cutting the two acres of grass with a smaller walk-behind mower. He said it got him in shape and he was feeling good physically.

About two weeks after getting home from the hospital, I got another abdominal pain. Pam called the cardiologist at the University Hospital to get his advice. He said for me to be taken all the way to the University Hospital (about 60 miles) by ambulance. With all the problems I had had, they didn't want to take any chances. After running some tests, they determined that my Gallbladder needed to be removed. After surgery, the surgeon who removed the Gallbladder told me that he had never seen a Gallbladder as bad as mine. He said it was green and black, totally dead, and that I was lucky to be alive. *God's hand in my life.*

SHEPHERDS CHAPEL (2004)

Sometime around 2004, my brother Dennis and I talked about our faith, as we had many times before. In this conversation, Dennis brought up the fact that he had been doing Bible study with a TV church called Shepherd's Chapel. He had mentioned them before but I had shown no interest. This time he kept saying I should try them out and that they touted the Three Earth Ages and it would help clarify much of the Bible. He described a bit of what he was talking about. This time I became a bit intrigued. He said he had some lessons on discs and he would send me a few to get me started.

When I first began watching the Shepherds Chapel Bible studies, I was not very impressed, but I had agreed to give it a couple weeks. By the middle of week two, I had a change of heart and began the study more intently. As I gained more exposure to the Bible study lessons, I began to understand things that had bothered me before in the Bible. I found that Shepherd's Chapel was on TV twelve or more hours a day, covering different lessons. Their live transmission was at 5 a.m., so I set up to record the live and a couple other times each day. Over a period of several months, I had the additional lessons I wanted and was into the Shepherd's Chapel study on a daily basis (they transmitted weekdays only).

Dennis was right, that the three Earth Ages made a lot of sense, tying in what happened originally with Lucifer's downfall (the first Earth Age) and the fall of man (the second Earth Age). These two ages lead to the third and last age when there will be a new Heaven and a new Earth.

I mentioned my satisfaction with the Bible Study to Pam, Joan and Jonathan. Pam wasn't interested, but Joan and Jonathan were. We started a collective Bible Study, getting together to watch lessons and discuss them. Eventually, we split up, with each of us doing the studies on our own time. I would make up discs from the recordings of each Bible Study book and provide Joan and Jonathan with copies.

One of the things I discovered with Shepherd's Chapel was that they covered the entire Bible, Old and New Testament, and I surprisingly found that the Old Testament has much of what is relevant today.

After a couple years or so, Joan, Jonathan and I began getting together to discuss our understanding of various Bible topics. These were great discussions and led to even creating quizzes for each other. Eventually, we lost interest and discontinued the discussions, but we all continued with our individual studies. At times, after that, Joan and I, or Jonathan and I would have impromptu discussions.

None of us were going to any churches. Since moving to Rush City, I had gone to several churches but never found one I wanted to stay at. I felt a desire but didn't find what I wanted. Shepherd's Chapel and my personal prayer life kept my life focused on Jesus. Also during this period, I was eager to learn all I could about God, Christianity, Religions, Angels, and many, many other related topics. I would pray for God to direct me to where I might learn more and, over the years, I was directed to a host of books, articles, religious programs and Web sites.

In the year 2000, at age 65 I retired. After retirement, I quit all my outside work. Pam was 8 years younger than I was, so it would be a while before she retired. In 2003, I realized that our bills were exceeding my income. Our medical insurance premiums were over $800 per month. I decided to get a job at the Walmart in Cambridge to help pay these medical premiums. I did this for five years. When Pam turned 65 in 2008, she retired. The cost of her health premiums dropped substantially so I quit Walmart.

PAM'S DEATH (2014)

Pam and I had been sleeping in separate beds for quite some time. My body produced so much heat that I could only use a sheet to cover me. On the other hand, Pam was usually cold. She liked sleeping together because I kept her nice and warm, but I was losing sleep, so we agreed to sleep in separate beds.

In November of 2013, Pam brought up the fact that our Van was getting old and it was a gas guzzler. We hardly ever used it. My pickup was our primary mode of transportation. I liked to drive, so most of the time we went together in the pickup. It was a good vehicle, especially in the snow, having a four-wheel drive that could be entered merely by stopping and changing a setting on the dash. I did some financial checking and discovered we could afford payments of up to $350 per month. I figured the van should provide the down payment, as long as we could stay under the $350 monthly limit, we were good to go.

We started looking at all kinds of cars but couldn't find what we wanted (or, in some cases, what we could afford). We did this for two weeks, and then realized that a new car seemed to be out of the question. I told her that we should pray about it and leave it in the Lord's hands.

The next morning, Pam told me she had the weirdest experience that night. She always watched some TV before going to bed, which she had done that evening. About two hours after turning off the TV, she was awakened by the TV being on. Not only that, it was on a different channel from when she had turned it off. She was about to turn it off when she heard a commercial from Friendly Chevrolet of a huge sale they were having. She said they were giving large discounts and zero percent financing. I told her she must have misunderstood. Dealers never give both zero percent financing and discounts, it is always one or the other. She insisted she heard right so we decided to go all the way to Blaine (about 40 miles) and visit them.

When we got there and spoke with a salesman, the first thing we did was ask about the combination discount with zero percent financing. He said it was true. They were offering that to qualified buyers (those with good credit ratings). On that basis we began looking at cars. Pam liked the Chevrolet Equinox. They had just received a shipment of 2014s. After picking out the one Pam liked best, we went for a test drive. It was going to be her car so she drove. She liked it but wanted me to drive it as well, so I did. We both liked the car. Next would be the haggling over a final price.

Our credit ratings were both excellent, hers slightly higher than mine. Since it was to be her car, we had them check her credit rating. After finding it was well into the 800s, they didn't hesitate to give us the zero financing and $7000 discount. We told them we had a custom van to trade in. The salesman's eyes lit up. He wanted to see it, so we took him out to the van. He was excited. He thought they could give us a good price but he would have one of their people check it out first. Pam and I had decided that if they offered $1500 for the van, we'd take the deal. A few minutes later, the salesman said they'd buy the van for $2500! We couldn't believe it. He also said we were in luck because that very day, Chevrolet had thrown in another $500 discount. When it was all said and done, we bought the car with an additional 100,000 maintenance policy on a zero percent five year loan for $345.71 per month. *God's hand in my life.*

The car was Pam's pride and joy. She drove it all the time. Since it got far better gas mileage, it was the vehicle of choice when we went out together.

Pam didn't like going to doctors. She was always making sure that I went, but she would nurse herself through colds and flu. She seldom got sick and seemed to have extra strength. We had two snow blowers. She would take one and I took the other. She would move up and down the long driveway faster than I could. She enjoyed outdoor work and felt it her duty to relieve me of as much as she could. Since I did all the wood processing for the house, it was her way of doing her share.

Pam had been complaining about night sweats for some time. She would wake up and her whole body was wet from sweat. I told her she should get it checked out, but she thought it was a passing thing. After a couple more weeks, with no improvement, she went to the doctor. Her doctor checked her for fever and found none. She suggested that Pam have a chest x-ray to see if there might be some kind of congestion causing the sweats. When the x-ray came back, the chest was clear but, at the very bottom, barely noticeable, was a black mass. She sent Pam down for x-rays of the abdominal area. We had things to do, so we left after the x-ray. Her doctor said if there was anything on the x-rays, she would call.

About an hour or so later, I got a call on my cell phone from her doctor. Pam and I were at Walmart in Forest Lake. Her doctor told me that Pam had a large mass in her abdominal cavity that looked like cancer. I told her doctor that she needed to tell Pam, so I gave her the phone. When we left the store, we were both in shock. We had the number of a cancer doctor at the University of Minnesota and made an appointment a few days later. On the way to the appointment, I drove and we talked a lot about our life together.

The cancer doctor confirmed that there was a large tumor, probably ovarian cancer, which needed to be removed as soon as possible. The doctor gave Pam hope of a full recovery with six Chemo treatments after surgery to remove any remaining cancer cells. Her surgery took over five hours. The doctor told me she removed a tumor the size of a football. After her recovery, Pam started weekly Chemo treatments, which affected her greatly. Pam would feel good for a day or two after the treatment, because of medication; once the medication wore off, she would feel weak and terrible for days. We found out after the third treatment that the cancer was growing in her body even with the treatment. They had kept that information from us. Pam was angry at not being told and said that she was stopping all further Chemo treatments.

While in the hospital after her last treatment, she was visited by a Palliative Nurse. It was she who told Pam the truth about her situation and that she only had a couple weeks to live. She took over Pam's care and asked Pam if she wanted to be in the hospital or at home during her remaining time. Pam said she wanted to be with her family at home. The nurse set up for Pam to receive Hospice services at home for the remainder of her time.

By this time, Pam could barely walk. She tried lying in her bed at home, but couldn't get in and out very easily. We had them order a hospital bed, which was delivered and set up in the living room the next day. During her remaining time, she was able to meet individually with every family member. She had family with her 24/7 until she passed on July 21, 2014. She did not want to have a funeral service but a cremation only.

The family held a private service at the home before her body was picked up for cremation. In one moment of time, I lost the love of my life, my best friend, my wife, the mother of my children, and a great companion. We had celebrated our 50th wedding anniversary on November 16, 2013. We had our ups and downs during the marriage, but I couldn't have picked a better mate. In fact, that last few years of our marriage was probably the best. Our relationship had become so close that we often completed each other's statements. She and I both enjoyed doing things for each other. God knew what He was doing when he had us meet so long ago at that bowling alley in Waukegan.

RESTORATION CHURCH (2014)

A few months after Pam's death, I received a piece of mail from a new church in Rush City. The church, called Restoration Church, had mailed out this simple flyer with hours of service, location and telephone number, inviting people in the area to join them in worship services on Saturday evenings or Sunday mornings. I remember laying the flyer down without giving it a second thought. Several days later I was clearing a stack of mail that had piled up on the kitchen table when I saw the church flyer once again. This time, for some reason, I read it more carefully and decided I should check out the church.

The following Sunday, I went to Restoration Church. At the door, greeting people was Penney Johnson, Pam and my doctor's nurse, whom I had known for many years. She greeted me and gave me a hug. It was at this time I discovered that her husband, Cary, was the pastor of this church. I met Cary that morning along with several church regulars. I was impressed by Cary's humility and his ability to speak plainly and emotionally in his sermon. I decided to have a one-on-one meeting with Pastor Cary to find out more about the church. During that following week, Pastor Cary and I met for lunch and got to know each other better. The Pastor answered all of my questions and, as we parted, said he hoped I would come to the church. My response was: "We'll see."

I started going to Restoration Church at the Saturday service and then got involved with a Bible Study group going through the book of Acts. The study was led by Paul Fry, one of the Elders of the church. The group had about eight or so people in it, including Bob Vanalstine, who I had known years before when he had a Barber Shop in North Branch where I got my hair cut regularly. Bob and I began meeting for lunches at Kaffe Stuga, a restaurant a few miles south of Rush City, in Harris. Over time we became close friends.

I felt the Lord directing me to get more involved with the church. The Worship Team consisted of Jim Anderson and Hannah Whittaker who both sang and played guitars. They were looking for people to join the team. One Sunday, Pastor Cary (who knew I played the Keyboard) came by where I was sitting and hinted that there was a need for a keyboardist. I decided to join the team, playing backup chording on the keyboard.

The Lord kept pushing me to find out what the needs of the church were. I met with Pastor Cary to talk about the church's needs. I started helping serve meals at the high school once a month. I enjoyed the interface with students coming through the line.

After church, one Sunday, I met with Drew Krech, an Elder at Restoration, to ask about the merits of having a Christmas Sing-a-Long at the church. He asked if I could put together my ideas and present it to the church board at one of their meetings. I put together a proposal that included a songbook handout with songs and interesting

Christmas trivia as well as church information. These were meant to be kept by people who would come to the Sing-a-Long. I wanted to have the Sing-a-Long early in December, before people became too busy with other things. The Pastor wanted Jim and Hannah to be there. Jim was out of town until later in December. The time was not what I wanted but I thought it was important to have the Sing-a-Long. The good thing is that it gave me more time to put together the songbook.

At Thanksgiving evening, several of the churches in Rush City have a combined service. My daughter Joan and I attended the service that year held at the Baptist church. It was a great time of hearing messages from various pastors and music from each church's worship team. Afterward, people congregated in the basement for refreshments and conversation. That evening I had a strong urge to discuss with Pastor Cary about the history of Restoration Church. He said he had always wanted to document it but never had the time. I told him I'd be glad to write the history, but I would need to talk to people who were involved along its history. We set up a meeting to talk more about it. At that meeting, Pastor Cary gave me names of people to interview about the church history. I told him I would start the process in January, since people were busy this time of year.

I began working on the Christmas Sing-a-Long, drafting a sample layout of the songbook for approval, and then researching appropriate songs for a one-hour program. Once the final draft was ready, I got approval from Pastor Cary and the church Elders. I then printed the songbook at home in the number of copies recommended. The Sing-a-Long went off as planned. Those who participated enjoyed the evening.

After the Christmas period, I began planning to do the church history. I wanted to meet with Pastor Cary and Penney first, since they would have the most to contribute. They would also provide me with the names of other people to contact about the history. As I began collecting information about the Restoration Church history, a pattern began to emerge, showing God's influence throughout the period. I wanted this to be evident in what I wrote so that the history itself would be a testimonial to God. I did sit-down interviews with as many key people as I could, taping each interview. The process worked well. Over the next couple of months I had a rough draft, which I provided to the Pastor for review and comment. I then finalized the history, providing a master copy to the Pastor for him to do with as he so chose.

Upon completion of the Restoration Church history, I began to feel less of a push from the Lord. I was beginning to have major health problems, causing me to drop out of the Worship Team, and to not participate in Bible Studies. I was going to church as often as I could. One time I mentioned to Pastor Cary if he had ever considered having people give testimonials at the church. I told him I would be glad to give mine as a starter. He liked the idea.

The Pastor and I did our testimonials the same day; he went first. Over time, they had several people give testimonials at the church. A few months later, the church had its first membership service. Since no one, not even the Pastor or the Elders were officially church members, they, as well as anyone else who accepted the Apostles Creed and were baptized as an adult in a fully immersed baptism, could join. Joan and I were among those who joined the church that day.

I must insert the fact that Joan, Jonathan and I had all received infant baptisms, several years earlier; the three of us did receive fully immersed baptisms in the swimming pool at the house. I pronounced the words over Joan and Jonathan, while fully immersing them one at a time, and Jonathan did the same for me.

I was beginning to be concerned about having to maintain the house. It was getting more and more difficult to do yard work. By this time Jonathan and Joan had begun receiving Social Security Disability Insurance (SSDI) income from the government. They were paying some toward monthly costs, but if I had a large bill, like a major repair or a major appliance to replace, I would have to bear most of the financial burden.

After examining my situation, and with a lot of prayer, I told them I would be selling the house and we all had to find a place to live. I wanted to be out of the house by fall because I did not want to go through another winter trying to keep the driveway clear. I was talking to Pastor Cary about my plans. He asked me to not put it on the market until his daughter, Brianna, talked to me. She was looking to move out of her apartment to a place for her and her two daughters. She also needed a place for her horse.

As time went on, it became obvious that the Lord was providing me with a buyer and Brianna with a home. It couldn't have been any better. There was a slight delay in setting the closing date, but that was also good. By the time I closed on the house, Joan, Jonathan and I had already found places to live and moved out. Brianna was able to come over and store things at the house before the closing, which helped her. My next move was to a senior apartment building in Chisago City.

CHISAGO CITY (2015)

In June of 2015, I moved into a senior apartment in Chisago City. It was interesting how this came about. Joan, Jonathan and I were all looking for apartments earlier this year. I had hoped that Joan and Jonathan would find their places first, reducing the concerns dealing with selling the house. Originally, the house was set to close in June; however, that got moved to July, giving me more time in preparing the house and getting rid of unwanted items.

I had gone to an apartment building in Chisago City earlier that year. I registered for a one bedroom with a den. The waiting list was several months at that time. I also looked at and registered at a couple other places. At the end of May, I received a call that a deluxe one bedroom apartment had just become available. I didn't know what a deluxe apartment was, but I didn't want to turn down any possibilities at this time.

I walked around the apartment and saw that it might work. The living room and bedroom were large. There were ample closets. Finally, the person giving me the tour, said, "By the way, there is a washer and dryer included." In a small room off the bathroom were a stacked washer and dryer. This convinced me to take the apartment, although it was expensive. The building was one level and they had many social activities, as well as a kitchen providing breakfast and lunch every day. My rent included one meal a day.

People from Restoration Church came on a Saturday and moved all my stuff in a matter of a few hours. Some of them even unpacked and set up my kitchen during this time. Not too long afterward, Joan and Jonathan found their places and were moved. *I can see God's hand in all of this.*

I liked the apartment. It had a large bay window in the living room that looked onto the beautiful landscaped grounds. The building was secure and very quiet. The only time I heard anything was if someone was walking by my door talking. I felt that the Lord wanted me there for a reason; I just needed to find out what it was. I prayed a lot about that.

I began meeting people, primarily at mealtime when I would sit with other tenants. I began playing my keyboard on a daily basis. I had not played regularly for some time and I needed the practice. Although I did not play the keyboard any louder than my TV, a next-door neighbor, who wears a hearing aid, said she could hear me playing music. She told me she went to bed at 8 p.m., so I told her I would quit playing before that time, which I did. People could hear me play as they walked by the door and would comment when they saw me that it was nice to hear the music.

I was having a lot of medical problems at this time, including heart palpitations, incontinence, neck and shoulder pains, and poor posture. I saw a Cardiologist at the University of Minnesota who informed me that I had an A-Fib condition which was usually treatable with beta blockers. My incontinence was primarily the inability to control urine, especially when I was cold. I would get an urgent need to urinate with no ability to control it. I wore a thick sanitary napkin, which helped treat the symptom but not the cause.

My doctor had an x-ray taken of the bladder to see if there might be a cause for my incontinence. What he found looked like bladder cancer. It was confirmed later by another doctor who scoped the bladder, showing me the cancer growth. I underwent surgery where the bladder was scraped to eliminate the cancer. The first scraping removed all the cancer from the inner wall, but the doctor discovered some cancer in the lining of the bladder. I received another scraping to remove that cancer. A three-month follow-up showed I was cancer free.

I have been checked several times since the surgery and continue to be cancer free. *God's hand in my life.*

Concerning my urinary incontinence, my Urologist prescribed a pill that would reduce the urgency, which it did. Over time I did not need the sanitary napkins.

The neck and shoulder pain and poor posture were related. An x-ray showed that I have a curved spine in my neck causing my neck and head to be bent forward. In the x-ray, it showed that my spinal cord was touching my spine at the bend. An operation to straighten the spine was out of the question. Because of my protruding head, my shoulder and back muscles ached. I received therapy concerning my neck, since, at this time, my neck and shoulders were in constant pain.

The shoulder and neck therapy helped somewhat, but the pain would come back. I prayed to the Lord concerning my neck and shoulder pain because it didn't seem to improve no matter what I did, and I often had to take pain killers to bring the pain down to a tolerable level. In a short time after my prayer, all shoulder and back pain went away, and stayed away. *God's hand in my life.*

Concerning my back pain, I have a wide back brace that helps support the muscles, so they do not weaken so quickly. Since the cause of the problem is the protruding neck and head, I am turning this over to the Lord as well.

I didn't see my neighbor very often, but every time I saw her, she would bring up about the keyboard. I would tell her that I no longer played after 8 p.m. and that I was not playing as loud as my TV. Regardless, she kept bringing up the same thing each time we met. One time when I was seated with a group of people for lunch she came over and right off said to everyone that she could hear me playing the keyboard. One of the ladies at the table said how lucky she was to hear that beautiful music. From all this I concluded that my neighbor was one of those who had to find something to complain about. One time she even pounded on the walls; this was 3:30 in the afternoon. I always thought it was interesting that she was hard of hearing, with hearing aids in her ears, but found my music too loud. As I am writing this, the thought just occurred that this might have been Satan's attempt at discouraging me from bring joy to others with my keyboard. It might also have been from the Lord to help in my future decision to move.

As I got better at playing the keyboard, I thought it would be good to play for the tenants. I set up to play every once in a while on Sunday during lunchtime. I did this for a while, but never felt it was what the Lord wanted.

MUSIC TRIVIA (2015)

Then one day I got the idea of having a Music Trivia activity once a month. The Activities Coordinator liked the idea, so it was set up for the first Friday of each month, at 10:00 a.m. in the Library. If we outgrew the Library, we could always have it in the dining room, since Friday meals were dinners instead of lunches.

I began preparing the Music Trivia sessions. It would consist of trivia about 20 songs that I would play. Each song was preceded by a question, such as: What was the name, or who made it famous, etc. I would then play the song through once, and then see if anyone was able to answer the question. My daughter, Joan, took care of the trivia part of the sessions, allowing me to concentrate on the music. After each trivia question was answered, Joan would then read a more in-depth music trivia item about the song. Some of the songs I had were sing-along. These sessions were well received, and it was a lot of fun.

After I was in the apartment a few months, I realized that I was being charged for my daily meal, whether I ate it or not. There was no credit for meals I did not eat. During this time I was missing over half of my meals because of medical appointments and menu items I could not eat. I brought this up with their management and was told that this was their policy; however, if I wanted to write a letter about my situation, they would be glad to review it. I prayed for guidance, talked to legal counsel about the matter, and drafted a letter. Legal counsel told me that the apartment owners could legally do what they were doing concerning the meals, even though it might not be morally correct.

A few days after this, the management of the apartment building issued a policy statement that credit would not be given for meals missed. They were even going to force people not on the meal plan to be on it. The tone of the statement told me to forget about the letter and begin looking for another place to live.

The first and only place I looked at was a large, 8-year-old apartment building in Forest Lake. It was ideally located with quick access to all parts of the city. It had two and three bedroom apartments, cheaper than where I was at, and the apartments came with washer and dryer. Although the building is three-level, it has a centrally located elevator and underground parking. An apartment became available one month before my year lease ended. I took it, and with the help of Joan, friends and a commercial mover, I was in my new apartment.

FOREST LAKE (2016-2017)

Although the apartment is not a senior building, I like it very much. It is large enough and is nearby to all the areas in downtown Forest Lake. The apartment is fairly peaceful and quiet. The only noise

I hear is the occasional running down the hallway by a younger person. Meeting people is more difficult because there is no commons area for get-togethers.

The Lord is giving me time to work on this writing. I also have time to continue with my music without fear of someone pounding on the walls or complaining every time I see them.

My body is getting weaker and more bent over. I have done all I can do in the way of medical support, such as prosthetics and exercises, which help, but do not provide any improvement. I am leaving it in the hands of the Lord whether he chooses to heal that portion of my body.

I am at peace here for the first time since before Pam died. It's a half-hour drive to Restoration Church. I go as often as my medical problems allow. I feel I should stay connected to the church; maybe the Lord still has use for me in that connection. Perhaps He has other plans for me. Whatever it may be is fine with me.

Summary

When I think back about my life, with its many twists and turns, I am humbled and awed at the same time. In my work history, I see a pattern of events, following my military experience, which led me throughout my career. Career moves were primarily related to training and training development, skills I acquired in the military. But then there was the diversion into radio and TV repair, which, at first, seems to have been a mistake. It helps me a lot to try and look at my life from God's perspective. This may seem ludicrous, but bear with me for a bit.

If I did an adequate job of describing the events leading to meeting and marrying Pam, the reader should agree that nothing preceding that meeting shows that I was heading in her direction, except for the little old lady in Philadelphia. Because of her prediction, and the fulfilling of it, I have to conclude that God was directing me toward Pam. He had selected her for me to marry. This may seem to be a pretty big step in faith, but I don't think so.

If it was God's goal to have Pam and I meet and get married, several things had to occur:

1. Eight years of my adult life had to pass to bring Pam to age 20. During that time I was getting a career started. Also, the many women who came into my life were each eliminated as a possible wife, some even against my will.
2. To meet Pam, I had to move to Waukegan. The sequence of job changes, leaving the Titan program, radio and TV repair, and then Philco, accomplished the move. First I should have stayed with Martin-Marietta. I didn't have to remain working at the missile silo; I could have transferred to other areas of the company; in fact, I was sent a letter from my former boss

at Martin-Marietta to come back, but I never responded. Buck's wife, Barb, didn't have to say anything about running the business at this time because we didn't have a business yet. The Philco job got me to Waukegan long enough to meet and marry Pam, and then the job disappeared. [Please do not think I believe that God did this for me only. I believe He uses events such as this to accomplish a multitude of goals. For example, my Best Man met his future wife because of his job change after Philco lost the contract. These things are impossible for us but simple for God.] Control Data hiring me and a host of other instructors the weekend after getting notice from Philco. Without the CDC job, I would not have married Pam. I would have wanted some form of income before getting married.

3. I had not bowled in Waukegan before meeting Pam. Something attracted me to be at the Dutch Doubles event. I went there to have a fun day, not to meet a girl.
4. There were a dozen or more bowling pairs at the Dutch Doubles. What were the odds of bowling against Pam?
5. Having been given the chance to meet Pam, I goofed up by not getting her telephone number or making a date to meet later. In spite of my failure, God in his patience gives me a second chance. This tells me He wanted us to get in a relationship.
6. Several weeks later, Pam bowls by herself, which she never did before, at the bowling alley where she had never bowled (she always bowled at the alley where we met). She could not explain (when we talked about it later) why she was there, except that she had a desire to bowl and decided to go to that bowling alley. She said she had asked her neighbor friend to go bowling (which they did frequently) but the friend was busy. Had her friend gone bowling with her, they would have gone to the other bowling alley. And let's not forget the timing. Pam could have bowled that day before or after the league was bowling, or, in fact, bowled any other time.

There is, I believe, a pattern to my various jobs. It seems that in most cases I remained in a job until circumstances forced a change or an opportunity came to me. Although I did not want to stay in the military, (my decision) had the Martin-Marietta job not appear virtually at the last minute, I would have reenlisted in the military. It was my decision to leave the Martin-Marietta job, but the reason disappeared (radio and TV repair) and if it had not been for the Philco job, my future would have been uncertain. I had put myself in a position of losing all the career benefits I had gained. When I look at the Philco job, it seems to have been (for me) primarily to meet and marry Pam. It did nothing for my career that I needed. I could have gone directly to Control Data from Massachusetts.

Many of my job changes within Control Data were opportunities that presented themselves at the right time. Going from instructing to heading up a Graphics Production department required me to take on production of the Basic Electronics textbook used by CDI. This was a new area to me. I had moved to CDI to teach; however, production of the textbook became my assignment. This led to forming a Graphics Production department, which became successful and fulfilled a growing need in the company, and a stepping stone for me.

I remember that in every management position I had in CDC, my budget was always just enough to meet the department's needs. I never exceeded any budget regardless of the fact that unanticipated changes occurred during the year. I remember year after year marveling at staying within budget even though there had been changes not included in the budget. It was when I acknowledged that God was behind my successes did I realize that He had kept my department within budget, not me.

Another example of God's involvement, I believe, was the Iran Program. Prior to CDC's contract another company had tried and failed. Several companies had been interested but when they examined the tasks involved, they all said it could not be done. After the project ended, I met with a person at the 3M Company who was the company's representative to a large educators group who collected and presented papers on advanced education topics. This person and I got to know each other quite well. We would meet monthly and discuss what was happening concerning education in our respective companies.

I had mentioned the past success of the Iran Program, that is, until the U.S. Embassy takeover. He was fascinated that we had succeeded because he had been in contact with the company that had tried and failed. He said that everyone who had looked at the tasks involved concluded that it was impossible. *When God is involved, nothing is impossible.*

Another project that I was involved with that was supposed to be impossible was when I was a consultant to Honeywell. Their Flight Control Systems division was moving to a new building. This involved 600 employees who had to learn new procedures, a new computer, and a host of new tasks, in addition to making the actual move, all in a six month period of time.

Although I had confidence in my abilities, I was encountering problems I had never faced before. I can remember the first time I was walking to my first meeting and praying to God that I have the wisdom and capability to do what was needed. They needed training on writing procedures. An employee of Honeywell had studied this area and created a basic training program. She had shown me what she had come up with and began the instruction, thinking I would join in. I was unaware and unprepared so she did all the training. Afterward she complained that I did not do my part. We met with the head of Human Resources and worked out our differences. After that, we got along very well and developed and presented a training program for management.

Honeywell managers would have to become instructors. They needed a Train-the-Trainer course, which I developed and taught. They needed to develop training materials. I helped them set up a graphics production shop to take care of their needs. We met, and in some cases, exceeded their expectations. The transition went off with only minor problems. I played my part, but it was God's involvement that mattered. Every time there was a major problem, along came a major solution.

To be born during the Great Depression, to a poor, struggling family, and, yet, to have been given the opportunities that have come along throughout my life, has been an amazing experience. To have been grounded in a strong work ethic from both my mother and father, to have been guided by Christian principles of honesty and compassion, to believe in myself, and to always remove emotions from decision making, as best I can, are among the many factors that have helped me be a successful manager.

Although I have health issues, God continues to have a hand in my life. Whatever He has in mind is okay with me. I hope that this book has been interesting and, in some way, helpful to you.

Endnotes

1 The **Samson AFB** facility was established initially by the United States Navy as a Naval Training Station (USNTS Sampson) in 1942. The station was named after Rear Admiral William T. Sampson. The Navy obtained 2,600 acres of former farmland and also vineyards for the facility on the east side of Lake Seneca, New York. The host organization at Sampson was redesigned as the 3650th Military Training Wing, Air Training Command, in March 1953. With the end of the Korean War and cutbacks in the military budget afterwards, Air Training Command discontinued its basic training school at Sampson AFB on 1 July 1956

(From Wikipedia, the free encyclopedia *Samson AFB)*

2 **Lowry Field** was named on 11 March 1938 for 2d Lt Francis Lowry, the only Colorado pilot killed in World War I combat. **Lowry Air Force Base** was designated on 24 June 1948 and on 26 August 1948 established all Lowry training organizations under the 3415th Technical Training Wing (redesignated "Lowry Technical Training Center" on 1 Jan 1959.

(From Wikipedia, the free encyclopedia *Lowry Field*)

3 The **Martin Marietta Corporation** was an American company founded in 1961 through the merger of Glenn L. Martin Company and American Marietta Corporation ...Martin, based in Baltimore, was primarily an aerospace concern with a recent focus on missiles, namely its Titan program. American-Marietta was headquartered in Chicago and produced paints, dyes, metallurgical products, construction materials, and other goods.

(From Wikipedia, the free encyclopedia *Martin Marietta*)

4 The **videotape format war** was a period of intense competition or "format war" of incompatible models of consumer-level analog video videocassette and video cassette recorders (VCR) in the late 1970s and the 1980s, mainly involving the **Betamax** and Video Home System (**VHS**) formats. **VHS** ultimately emerged as the preeminent format.

(From Wikipedia, the free encyclopedia, *Videotape format war*)

[5] The **Iran hostage crisis** was a diplomatic standoff between Iran and the United States. Fifty-two American diplomats and citizens were held hostage for 444 days from November 4, 1979, to January 20, 1981 after a group of Iranian students belonging to the Muslim Student Followers of the Imam's Line, who supported the Iranian Revolution, took over the U.S. Embassy in Tehran. It stands as the longest hostage crisis in recorded history.

(From Wikipedia, the free encyclopedia, *Iran hostage crisis.*)

CPSIA information can be obtained
at www.ICGtesting.com
Printed in the USA
LVHW091251040319
609409LV00001B/6/P

9 781643 612195